Paul Strebel

Steven Carvell

IN THE SHADOWS
OF WALL STREET
A Guide to Investing
in Neglected Stocks

PRENTICE-HALL, INC.
Englewood Cliffs, New Jersey 07632

Library of Congress Cataloging-in-Publication Data

Strebel, Paul.
   In the shadows of Wall Street.

   Bibliography: p.
   Includes index.
   1. Stocks—United States.   2. Investments—United
States.   3. Stock-exchange—United States.   I. Carvell,
Steven.   II. Title.
HG4921.S84 1988   332.63'22   87-42680
ISBN   0-13-455999-1

To all those who remained in the shadows while we wrote this book.

Editorial/production supervision and
   interior design: *Nancy Menges*
Cover design: *Lundgren Graphics, Ltd.*
Manufacturing buyer: *Lorraine Fumoso*

The publisher offers discounts on this book when ordered
in bulk quantities. For more information, write:

Special Sales/College Marketing
Prentice-Hall, Inc.
College Technical and Reference Division
Englewood Cliffs, New Jersey 07632

Printed in the United States of America
10   9   8   7   6   5   4   3   2   1

ISBN   0-13-455999-1   025

PRENTICE-HALL INTERNATIONAL (UK) LIMITED, *London*
PRENTICE-HALL OF AUSTRALIA PTY. LIMITED, *Sydney*
PRENTICE-HALL CANADA INC., *Toronto*
PRENTICE-HALL HISPANOAMERICANA, S.A., *Mexico*
PRENTICE-HALL OF INDIA PRIVATE LIMITED, *New Delhi*
PRENTICE-HALL OF JAPAN, INC., *Tokyo*
PRENTICE-HALL OF SOUTHEAST ASIA PTE. LTD., *Singapore*
EDITORA PRENTICE-HALL DO BRASIL, LTDA., *Rio de Janeiro*

CONTENTS

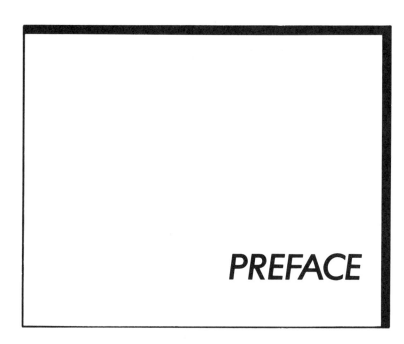

PREFACE

Every investor has a unique style. Investors differ not only as individuals, but also in terms of investment experience. Thus, optimists are more bullish than pessimists, and those caught at the peak of a market cycle are more cautious the second time around. Having unique experience, each investor applies a unique mix of criteria when making investment decisions. In practice, there are as many different styles of investment decision making as there are minds that apply themselves to it.

The intriguing thing, however, is that beneath the surface of all the styles lies a mere handful of basic investment theories. Their disciples can be grouped into four categories: technicians, fundamentalists, academicians, and contrarians. The argument and method expounded in this book can be more easily understood if it is seen against the backdrop of these four basic investment theories.

At the heart of technical theory is the simplest and most fundamental of all investment axioms: Buy low and sell high. The trick, of course, is how to tell when the index or security is at a low or a high. Here innumerable guidelines and trigger points enter. Most reflect the charting and analysis of a time series of price or volume data. The more sophisticated are based on statistical measures of the shifts in underlying supply and demand for the security in the market.

Fundamental theory is based on economic analysis at the macro level and valuation methods at the micro level. Fundamentalists employ a range of economic theory, from sophisticated econometrics to mundane platitudes in attempts to anticipate the market's movement. To paraphrase Keynes, many practical decisions are based unwittingly on the theories of economists, long since dead. In the case of valuation methods, it was the work of Graham and Dodd which set the tone more than thirty years ago with the development of a systematic approach to financial statement analysis: In the simplest of terms, buy when the security is undervalued and sell when it is overvalued.

Academicians follow the principles developed by business school economists. In the early nineteen-sixties, the Chicago School formulated the so-called *efficient market hypothesis*. Since all available information, both technical and fundamental, is already reflected in share prices, they argued, it is pointless to try and outperform the market averages. The best strategy is to put together a portfolio representative of the market as a whole. This passive approach has attracted a sizable band of investors disillusioned with the activist models.

Finally, there are the contrarians. Their philosophy is best summarized by the Baron de Rothschild, who is reputed to have said, "The best time to buy real estate is when there is a revolution in the streets." The contrarians take the view that the only possible way of beating the market averages is to do the opposite of what is suggested by the market consensus or majority view. A vast array of practical approaches have been put forward as representative of the contrarian method, claiming some of the best investment performance. However, no coherent theory has yet emerged to provide a rational economic basis for contrarian strategy.

These basic investment theories differ primarily in terms of the information they use to anticipate price movements. The technicians focus on short-term price and volume movements relative to historical patterns. The fundamentalists regard underlying economic information as key to future price movements. Academicians believe prices adjust almost instantaneously to reflect new information, so that neither technical nor fundamental information has any practical value. And the contrarians employ an eclectic, at times entrepreneurial, approach to information processing.

This book is in the contrarian tradition. It provides a rational basis for and a systematic approach to contrarian-type strategies. Its genesis occurred in the discovery of the *neglected firm effect:* Stocks neglected by security analysts provide much better returns than those that are followed. On the surface, the implication of the neglected firm effect is that investors may be better off without analysts. This apparently surprising result, in fact, represents some of the best evidence in favor of contrarian strategies. Even more important, the explanation of the neglected firm effect provides a rigorous basis for a practical approach to active investment.

While there are four basic investment theories, there are really only two practical investment approaches. The first is to take a random walk down Wall Street in the tradition of the academic school. The investor selects a diversified portfolio of securities and accepts whatever returns the market averages offer. The concentration of analyst attention and security research on popular stocks and market segments places these in the information spotlight. The competition for information around such better-known stocks is so intense that it is virtually impossible to use fundamental or technical analysis to develop a consistent investment advantage relative to the market indices.

The second practical approach to investment, which is the subject of this book and at the heart of most contrarian strategies, is to invest in the shadows of Wall Street. The investor avoids the information spotlight by concentrating on unpopular securities that are not heavily researched by analysts and followed by institutions. The competition for information around these securities is much less intense. The investor has a much better chance of employing fundamental analysis and, in a special way, technical analysis to beat the market averages.

However, there are no quick fixes. This book does not contain a magic formula for investment success that can be applied without effort. Today's security markets are far too sophisticated for such formulas, if they exist, to last long enough to be described in print. Wise investors are wary of the Ponce de Leon complex and remember the Mississippi Scheme, the South Sea Bubble, and the Dutch Tulip Mania, not to mention innumerable other schemes and investment books that have promised the impossible, swallowed the investor's funds, and delivered nothing.

Investing is no different from other economic activity in that consistent success requires effort. The key question is where that effort should be directed, where the chances for success are greatest. The basic argument in this book is that investors and portfolio managers have by far the best chances of beating the market averages, not in the informational spotlight, but in the shadows. The book provides evidence of the superior returns that investors and portfolio managers can expect if they put their investment effort into the shadows rather than the spotlight. In practical terms, it outlines how neglected stocks can be identified and what kind of research is most appropriate in the shadows.

Part I examines the situations that investors and portfolio managers can expect to encounter in the shadows. Special attention is given to the more rigorously documented reports of contrarian-type investment anomalies. The basic argument is that these are not separate effects: virtually all of them reflect the relative lack of information in the shadows.

In contrast to Part I, which is conceptual and analytical in tone, Part II is more practically oriented. Metaphorically, Part II shows how the shadows can be pierced by security research. It provides a systematic approach to the selection of undervalued neglected stocks, with a focus on the five key steps involved. The emphasis is on how standard security analysis is best modified for application in the shadows. Chapters 5, 6, and 7, which concentrate on the application of fundamental methods to the shadows, are somewhat more complex; readers not familiar with the use of such methods in the spotlight may want to merely skim these chapters on a first reading, so as not to interrupt the flow of ideas.

Part III examines how individual stock selection can be integrated into the development of a shadow investment strategy, either as a unique strategy or as part of a larger investment portfolio. Finally, in the appendix, the perspective shifts briefly from that of the investor, or portfolio manager, to that of the corporate treasurer managing the information cost of financing in the shadows.

This book is not intended for the faint of heart. It is written for those who put time into investing—active individual investors, portfolio managers, brokers, fund managers, corporate treasurers, all those in the professional investment community. For the first time it brings together the key evidence on investment return anomalies, including neglected stocks, small capitalization stocks, low P/E stocks, discount stocks; it shows how the biggest payoff to security research occurs not in the spotlight but in the shadows; and it provides a systematic guide to the methods that are most useful for investing in neglected stocks. Like sustained investment success that requires effort, the full benefit of these ideas and frameworks can only be had by committed reading. However, the book is written in a straightforward style, jargon has been kept to a minimum, and references and statistical details have been banished from the text to the bibliography. As a result, we hope that it will be accessible, and of interest to all active investors.

ACKNOWLEDGMENTS

This book had its genesis in the discovery of a neglected firm effect, together with Avner Arbel of Cornell University. Avner's challenging ideas and infectious enthusiasm were a source of constant inspiration and motivation. The first article on the neglected firm effect provoked comment in many parts of the financial media and press, including the *Wall Street Journal, Business Week,* and *Fortune.* The comments that affected our thinking most were those made by James B. Cloonan of the American Association of Individual Investors, whose metaphor of shadows and spotlight we adapted into the unifying theme of the book. While integrating the notion of neglected stocks into the wider tapestry of investment ideas, we received continual encouragement and open comment from Alex Gould of the Institutional Brokers Estimate Service. Their data tapes played an integral part in our later work, reflected in a number of published articles that we co-authored.

The earlier analysis was done while on the Binghamton Campus of the State University of New York, which provided us with a supportive environment, all the necessary facilities, and several research grants. The synthesis took place for one of us at IMEDE, the International Management Development Institute in Switzerland, and for the other, at Bentley College in Massachusetts and at Cornell University in New York. The practice-oriented environment at IMEDE and Cornell was a continual spur to ensure the professional relevance of everything in the book. In addition, IMEDE was especially generous with typing and graphical assistance. Michelle de Marval did the lion's share of the typing, and Michele Mayer created all the graphs. Special thanks are also due to Dean Jack Clark, of the Cornell University School of Hotel Administration, who supplied grant money and support that allowed the authors to complete the final editing of the book.

Finally, our association with the publisher, Prentice-Hall, has been a very positive one and we are especially grateful to our editors, Jeffrey Krames and Nancy Menges, for the constructive way they have nurtured this book into being.

PART I

SHADOWS
OF NEGLECT

This section describes how differences in available information affect the nature of investment. The contrast between the information spotlight and the shadows is explored in Chapter 1 in terms of the information demanded by investors and supplied by analysts. The impact of information differentials on investment returns is discussed in Chapter 2, which shows how the neglected firm effect dominates the other return anomalies in the shadows. Chapter 3 examines the logic behind the shadow effect, in order to determine whether the available price discounts can be exploited to beat the market averages.

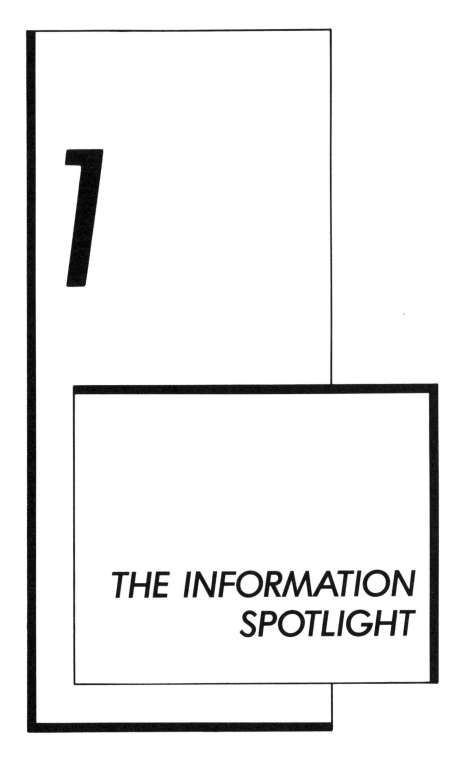

1

THE INFORMATION
SPOTLIGHT

What drives investment performance? Is there really anything more to it than chance? How useful is the information produced on Wall Street? What determines the focus of analysts' attention? These are some of the questions which are addressed in this chapter as we explore the supply and demand for investment information and, in particular, what draws attention to certain stocks rather than others.

IS THE STOCK MARKET A CASINO?

Many a disgruntled investor has said that playing the market is like playing Vegas: "There's no point thinking about it, you just do it." When things are going well, investors' theories seem invincible. But when things turn sour, making money in the market is reduced to a matter of luck. All the analysis and commentary churned out by the investment community is merely hoopla with little, if any, real value.

Disgruntled investors have good company. Literally hundreds of rigorous academic studies have demonstrated, apparently, that it is impossible to beat the market averages consistently for any length of time. The larger stock exchanges, no matter where in the world, are said to be efficient in the sense that all publicly available information is immediately reflected in stock prices. New analytical techniques are rapidly imitated, so that it is virtually impossible to develop a sustainable investment advantage. Attempts to beat the market averages are a matter of chance and, in that sense, no different from the roll of a dice.

Business school academics would contend, in addition, that the impossibility of anticipating the average of millions of expectations suggests that the optimal strategy is to buy a portfolio of stocks representative of the market as a whole. In so doing, investors can reduce their transaction costs by buying an index fund, for example, and accepting whatever return the market offers.

On the other hand, investment professionals would argue that Las Vegas differs from Wall Street both in process and content. In Las Vegas, each throw of the dice is completely independent from the previous one. The number that comes up has nothing to do with the croupier. It doesn't depend on the players' information: what they know is irrelevant. The stock market, on the other hand, is locked into investors' expectations about the future, companies' performance, and the economy as a whole. While these expectations can fluctuate sharply, the economy cannot change completely overnight. Although expectations may move randomly, there is an underlying economic reality, linked from one day to the next by business structures and processes.

The market can be said to play a central role in the economy by providing continuous feedback on the average investor's expectations. It is one of the key leading indicators of future economic performance. The stock market highlights those industries and segments which are thought to have good prospects, where capital investment by firms is most likely to pay off. In fact, some commentators have suggested that socialist economies could employ their best economic minds far better by having them play "stock exchange," rather than by having them draw up five-year plans. The capitalist stock exchanges, where participants put dollars behind their forecasts, are said to be much closer to economic reality than the Kremlin schemes of socialist planners.

Investment professionals might say, moreover, that the hypothesis of so-called market efficiency is academically interesting but practically irrelevant. If it were relevant, all rational investors would have converted their portfolios into index funds long ago. Most investment advisors and portfolio managers would have been forced into early retirement. Clearly, there are a lot of investors who either are irrational or have yet to buy the idea. Besides, if the analysts and fund managers stopped doing security research, there's no way the market could function properly. Investors would be forced to guess firm values, in the process making large estimation errors resulting in wide price fluctuations. Therefore, analysts' information plays a critical role in the pricing process, allowing investors to zero in on an appropriate price.

The important point is that, despite the apparent gap between these caricatures of the academic and professional investment views, they are two sides of the same coin. Academics tend to be concerned mainly with the evaluation of existing information. Many of the recent breakthroughs in valuation methods have originated in academia, the analysis of portfolio risk, arbitrage pricing theory, and the option valuation formulas being some of the better-known examples. By the same token, the efficient market hypothesis is really concerned with the relationship between prices and information at equilibrium: Given the available information, what is the level of stock prices? It says nothing about the process whereby information becomes available, nothing about the market for information.

By contrast, the professional approach to investment is very much concerned with the information collection process. The analyst, portfolio manager, or broker is frequently the agent who makes information publicly available. Survival depends on the ability to access and/or analyze information before it becomes widely known. Rather than a precise valuation model, the analyst or broker is interested in new information, simply because this is the best available indicator of which way prices will move. For them the market is rarely at equilibrium. Survival dictates that they continually find new information to maintain their competitive advantage and increase their customer base. Thus, the analyst is constantly involved in the dynamic competition for information which creates the tendency toward equilibrium.

As always, the key question is whether one can beat the market averages. Are the academics right in contending that the investment game is no more than a random walk down Wall Street? Or can it be convincingly demonstrated that abnormal returns are possible, that the market averages can be consistently beaten? If so, is this true of all stocks, or is it in any way linked to the information acquisition and processing which takes up so much of the professionals' time? Before we can answer these questions, we need to be clearer about what we mean by information—the nature of the demand for it on the one hand, and its supply on the other.

DEMAND FOR INVESTMENT INFORMATION

Information is a message shedding light on the possible forms of an uncertain event. Consider an investor, for example, who anticipates three types of market conditions, bullish, bearish, and stagnant, each with equal probability. For this investor and this set of outcomes, information is any data which sharpens his prediction by altering the probabilities associated with the different outcomes, making a bullish market more likely, say. To the extent that some outcomes are considered more probable than others, the uncertainty surrounding the future state of the market has been reduced.

The quantity of information in the message can be specified in terms of the corresponding reduction in uncertainty.

The key point for our purposes is that information is not the same as data. One can talk about the quantity of data in terms of the physical amount of it, computer bits, pages of a report, and so on. But the amount of information in the data is another matter. It depends on the content of the message, the extent to which it reduces uncertainty. We may have reams of data but zero information, unless the data changes the chances we associate with the different market conditions in our example.

Once information is received, what is its value to the investor? The value of the information about the greater likelihood, say, of a bullish market depends on three factors: first, whether the investor can understand the message and believes it; second, whether the investor can take any action based on the information; and third, what net benefits would accrue from the actions taken. We shall consider briefly each of these in turn.

Credibility of Information

If the investor cannot understand the message, it is worthless. Information on the research projects of a high-tech firm is of little value to someone who is not familiar with the industry. Similarly, when the savings and loan segment of the banking industry was deregulated in the United States, there was initially very little information and analysis, until the economics of the industry were better understood.

If the investor comprehends, but the information runs counter to his prior beliefs, he may completely ignore it, regardless of the potential. The latter situation is very familiar, the tendency to see and believe what one wants to believe. Psychologists use the term *cognitive dissonance*. And it isn't necessarily purely psychological. The room for error in a lot of market information and opinion makes it rationally prudent to await confirmation before acting on, say, the forecast of a single analyst who is challenging the consensus view. Nobody knows much about how investors, or decision makers in general, absorb information, how much evidence they need to change their opinion. All that can be said is that the credibility of information is critical to its value.

Constraints on the Investor

If the information is credible, the next question is what action can be taken. Bullish market data has no value to someone who is penniless. The best information received by the most brilliant mind is worthless unless the receiver can access the resources needed to act on the information. The value of investment information depends, therefore, on the funds that can be potentially controlled by the investor. Financial institutions managing billions of dollars employ in-house analysts to follow companies in which they have large holdings. Even a small percentage change in anticipated return has a significant dollar value for such large shareholders. Needless to say, institutions react quickly to changes in perceived value and play a dominant role in pricing decisions.

Despite large holdings, investment action may be restricted by legal and other constraints. Information is less valuable for securities which are out of bounds for any reason. For example, the pressure against investment in South Africa has made information on African gold shares much less valuable to American investors. Another example is implicit in the appraisal system used to evaluate the performance of investment managers. Insofar as below-average performance is more heavily penalized than superior performance is rewarded, managers tend to shy away from risky securities. This reduces the value of investment information pertaining to these types of stock.

A key variable is the individual's aversion to risk. Investors can be highly heterogeneous in the utility they associate with information. Low-income investors cannot afford to take on much financial risk. Therefore, like portfolio managers with risk-avoiding incentives, they tend to avoid highly uncertain positions. As a result, the first information on the changing performance of a risky company, for example, is of varying value to different investors. Many individuals want confirmation of the information before they make an investment decision.

Net Benefits of Information

Even if the investor is able and willing to act, the value of information finally depends on the benefit, net of transaction costs, of whatever decisions might result from the information. Thus, the information on the possibility of a bullish market suggests a set of investment decisions with an expected net benefit. The value of the information on a bullish market is equal to the change in net worth anticipated by the investor.

Information timing may be equally as important to investors as information content. The first credible information on a new situation usually has the greatest investment value. Often communicating the basis of the event, the range of likely outcomes, it has the greatest impact on uncertainty. Examples include the flash money supply, or leading indicator announcements at the macro level, or earnings figures at the corporate level. Later information tends to refine the detailed aspects of the forecast, with correspondingly less impact on the uncertainty faced by investors.

Who gets the information first is even more critical for investment purposes. As James Rogers, the founder of the Quantum Fund, puts it: "I try to find the things that are going to change and I try to figure out long before other people." Being the first to spot an opportunity, or to evaluate its potential, gives an investor the best chance of getting in or out at the right price. This is especially true in efficient markets where prices adjust rapidly to new information. Most of the research indicates that in the largest markets with tightly knit networks of analysts, brokers, and traders, the adjustment is very rapid, occurring within hours, if not minutes, for certain kinds of information. What happens in the shadows, however, where the network may be thin with very few participants, is much less clear-cut.

Declining Returns to Information

Taking these two factors together, the information sequence and who gets it first, suggests that a kind of 80/20 rule is probably at work: The first 20 percent of the information on a particular situation or opportunity generates 80 percent of the investment value; the last 80 percent of the information on the subject is worth only 20 percent of the total value. In economic language, this amounts to declining returns to information. Since, in general, there are declining returns to most resources, it is hardly surprising that the same should be true for information.

The notion of declining returns to information is crucial, because it underlines the value of information regarding significant change that has occurred. For any particular investor, information is most valuable when the investment situation has changed and uncertainty is high. It becomes less and less valuable as more and more information arrives and the uncertainty is resolved. When the situation has been stable for a time, additional information has very little value. For example, when a company has reported poor results for several quarters, more information on what is already known to be a bad situation has little value, unless a significant turnaround is in the offing.

The above discussion on the nature of the demand for investment information can be summarized as follows: Investors place a higher value on

- Information they can relate to, on companies, industries, or markets about which they already know something.
- Information which is credible, confirmed by several sources, or coming from a reliable source.
- Information on which action can be taken, not ruled out by institutional constraints, the investor's risk aversion, or a lack of funds.
- Information which they are the first to receive and/or which arrives first, on a new or changed opportunity.

Conversely, unconfirmed information on unknown, risky companies, as well as continual information on known companies with stable earnings, is of little value to investors in general. The small incremental return on such information for most investors has important implications when considered together with the supply side of the information-generating process.

SUPPLY OF INVESTMENT INFORMATION

What investors want in terms of information, analysts may not be willing to provide. The amount of information which analysts and others in the investment community are willing to supply depends on what it costs to produce versus what investors will pay. Provided that there are enough investors for whom the value of the information is greater than the production cost, the information will be supplied. Several factors affect the cost of producing investment information.

Information Cost Factors

Consider first, not necessarily in order of importance, corporate disclosure policy. The spirit of disclosure varies widely across companies, despite the disclosure requirements imposed on U.S. firms by the SEC and other statutory bodies. Some companies provide information on factors critical to security pricing, such as future investment plans, anticipated returns, and risk, while others restrict themselves to historical reporting. Clearly, the greater the corporate disclosure, the less the cost of security research.

Another factor determining the cost of investment information has to do with economies of research scope. Analysts can develop economies of scope by following groups of companies, usually in the same or related industries. Information on one firm is useful in analyzing another, especially when they are competitors. Even if they are not, overlapping activities make it simpler to put strategic moves into context. Economies of research scope can also arise out of the exchange of information between analysts with similar interests. Here, of course, there is the danger of a herd effect developing, as analysts follow one another in developing their opinions.

The quality of the research also clearly affects its cost. The better the analyst, the greater is the opportunity cost of his or her time. Really valuable investment research is not that common. Knowing how to pick up the relevant information from the mounds that are disseminated by the media and come across every analyst's desk is an art in itself. As Donald B. Kurtz, chairman and chief executive officer of Equitable Investment Management, points out,

"The process of gathering information has been developed to a unprecedented level. It's just like watching a fast movie screen running before your eyes. The trick, the skill, the ability, is to be able to pull back from the mass of information; (and) decide which information is relevant." Understanding the economics and dynamics of an industry, as well as the position and potential of the key players, is no simple task. When the finesse of timing is added to the analyst's brew, it is no wonder that top-class security analysts are rare.

Whether analysts will supply the information on a security, in the final analysis, depends on whether sufficient investors will pay enough to cover the total production cost. The number of investors interested in a particular piece of security research is closely related to the breadth of the investor base. The economies of security research are more attractive when the investment base is broad, mainly because the analysts are more assured of covering their fixed costs. Large but otherwise uninteresting public utilities, for example, often have several analysts covering them, because the wide investor base makes it possible to sell enough of even low-value information to break even.

Comparative Advantage of Analysts

What individual investors are willing to pay, however, is limited by the cost of do-it-yourself security research. If portfolio managers can do the research on a particular company more cheaply, they may not be so readily disposed to buy it on the outside. A reasonably experienced and focused analyst with a support network should be able to do research of a comparable level more economically than investors who manage a large portfolio or have other employment. But when a company is very secretive, when very little is disclosed no matter what the researcher's affiliation, the professional analyst has a much smaller comparative advantage. Similarly, when a situation is static with little happening, the absence of complexity and change reduces the analyst's advantage.

More importantly, analysts have difficulty matching the information of insiders. Although inside information cannot be traded upon legally, investors who have an intimate knowledge of an industry or companies, without being insiders in the legal sense, can often obtain and assess critical information more readily than analysts. The superior performance of true insiders has been documented quite extensively. Academic researchers argue that insiders are the only investors likely to achieve consistently superior returns. Apparent confirmation of this view is provided by the ever-tightening legal noose around insider trading.

In brief, the supply of investment information will tend to be greater:

- The lower the production cost; that is, the greater the corporate disclosure, the greater the overlap with other companies, and the lower the opportunity cost of the analysts' time.
- The greater the comparative advantage of analysts versus do-it-yourself investor research, which is greater for complex and dynamic situations, like conglomerates and companies in rapidly evolving industries.
- The larger the number of potentially interested investors.

Finally, there is the possibility that self-employed analysts might decide to trade on their own analysis rather than sell it. The attraction of using one's own security research is a function of the net investment benefit perceived by the analyst, versus the price which the research will fetch in the marketplace for information. However, the market price of information depends on the interaction between its demand and supply, an issue to which we now turn.

INFORMATION SHADOWS

A critical question for this book is whether information is equally available across securities, whether the spotlight of analysts' attention can be expected to fall equally across securities. Several factors on both the information demand and supply sides indicate the very opposite, that the equilibrium level of analysts' attention will vary dramatically. This can be seen by pulling common themes out of the discussion on information supply and demand.

Impact of Firm Size

An obvious common factor affecting both the supply and demand for information is size, or the market capitalization of a company. On the supply side, size is a key cause of differential security information. Large companies can support a much wider investor base than small firms. Numerous shareholders translate into many potential users of security research, making it easier for analysts to sell their services at a competitive price.

On the demand side, financial institutions cannot easily invest in firms with small capitalizations. The typical size of an institutional investment may affect the price and, hence, the liquidity of low-capitalization securities. In addition, an institution's holding may become so large that it necessitates managerial input, which falls outside the institution's area of interest and expertise. Moreover, institutional fund managers may be constrained by their incentive systems to be risk averse; they are expected to be prudent and cannot take the greater risk frequently associated with small companies.

In the absence of institutional investors, therefore, small companies are held by private investors, whose holdings in many cases are not large enough to support expensive security research. Thus, for both demand and supply reasons, large-capitalization firms often attract analysts and are in the spotlight, whereas small firms tend to find themselves in the information shadows.

Profile of Firms in the Spotlight

Of course, there's much more to it than size alone. Looking back at the summaries of the factors influencing information demand and supply, we see that two polar corporate profiles emerge, corresponding to companies in the spotlight and those in the shadows. In the spotlight, firms are experiencing change—the more dramatic, the stronger the spotlight. Any information on them is valuable to investors on the demand side. Professional analysts on the supply side have a strong comparative advantage over do-it-yourself research, owing to the complexity thrown up by most change. A necessary condition for attention is that the firms be willing to disclose relevant information, within the reasonable bounds imposed by product competition. The spotlight tends to pick up such companies more rapidly, especially if there is overlap with other heavily followed companies, or if the company is more visible for other reasons.

Consequently, even small companies may get a lot of attention when they break new ground in terms of product or industry development. A classic example is that of Apple Computer, which from its earliest days understood how dramatization of its product could be used not only to build sales, but also to develop a following in the financial community. In the words of Pamela Bayless of the Institutional Investor, Apple uses extravaganzas "complete with glaring spotlights and loud music," to introduce new products to analysts and the press.

Profile of Firms in the Shadows

By contrast, companies in the shadows are out of sight to investors and/or uneconomical to research for analysts. Out of sight often means unknown, or difficult to relate to. Even large companies can fall into this category. For example, the Europe-based Unilever, one of the twenty largest industrial companies in the world, was relatively unknown in the United States before it began its investor relations effort in 1979. Several years of presentations and visits to security analysts and their meetings made only a small impact on the company's U.S. following. The American investment community had difficulty comparing Unilever to its North American competitors, until a meeting at Unilever House itself in London featured conferences with top management and explanations of Unilever's strategy. Thereafter, the company came out of the shadows into the spotlight with a dramatic increase in analysts' coverage, number of U.S. shareholders, and share price.

Highly secretive corporations are found in the information shadows. Here again, large firms may be involved, especially if they are mainly family held, or have a tradition of minimal disclosure, which is frequently the case in Europe, for example. While information on such companies may be very valuable to investors, it is often impossible for analysts to get their hands on anything, beyond the little which investors already know. The famous grain merchants, the seven sisters who control the international grain trade, fall into this category. The secrecy surrounding their activities makes it difficult for analysts to add anything to the existing speculation about their prospects.

Finally, and possibly most importantly, when a company is in the doldrums for a long period of time, it tends to drift into the shadows, because there is very little new information of value. Mature firms in mature industries are susceptible to this kind of neglect. Information on their slowly changing situations does not have much value. When analysts cannot sell the information, they stop researching the companies. Thus, companies with continual lackluster results over an extended period are often ostracized by the investment community.

Existence of the Shadows

The existence of information shadows, the first contention of this chapter, is beyond doubt. The actual research coverage of securities by analysts confirms this point. Within the Standard and Poors list of 500 large U.S. companies, in 1976 for example, approximately one-half of analysts' attention was devoted to about one-fourth of the companies. Close to a quarter of their attention was focused on the five most heavily researched companies, while five percent received almost no regular coverage. Beyond the S&P 500, the research coverage declined very rapidly. This particular survey conducted by Drexel Burnham Lambert was based on at least two-thirds of the analysts with U.S. market influence. With respect to size, another study of analysts' coverage of the S&P 500 found that of the largest 30 percent of the companies, a quarter were neglected by analysts in the sense that their coverage was very light relative to the rest of the sample.

No matter what proxy measure is used for the information available on a security, the variation in the intensity of the spotlight is great. For example, an analysis of the number of institutions holding the stock of a random sample of 510 companies drawn equally from the New York Stock Exchange, the American Stock Exchange, and the over-the-counter markets, during the 10-year period 1971 to 1980, found that one-third of the companies in the sample were neglected by financial institutions; that is, held by just one, or by no institutions at all.

Durability of the Shadows

The second contention of this chapter, that the shadows will always be well populated, is immediately evident from the economics of security research described above. For the shadows to disappear, all firms would have to be continually researched by many analysts. Analysts would have to follow all companies regardless of how uninteresting their earnings patterns might be, how small, secretive, or complex they might be. It is difficult to imagine how profit-maximizing analysts could rationalize following such companies.

Moreover, the quest for personal security makes analysts vulnerable to a herd effect that causes them to shift in unison from one type of company to another as corporate prospects fluctuate over time. These analyst fads seem to be based on the sector of the economy likely to perform best in the near future. Domestic oil stocks, for example, were all the rage when oil prices skyrocketed in the 1970s, but faded when the price stabilized and declined in the early 1980s. Similarly, the high-tech stocks have tended to lead off recent economic and stock market upswings. But attention shifts to more mature companies as the upswings gather momentum, and so on. The switching of analysts' attention is basically a reflection of the ever-present cycles in economic activity. As long as economic cycles exist, there will be highly uneven coverage of the market by analysts and hence relatively neglected stocks even among large companies.

Companies also come and go. Moving through their life cycle in phases, companies undergo change and attract attention at different times. The 50 highest-growth blue chip corporations today are not the same as those of twenty years ago. According to Beatrice Garcia of the *Wall Street Journal*, "Stocks making their 1986 debut on the 'new nifty 50' lists include Cray Research, Deluxe Check Printers, Federal Express, General Cinema, Limited Stores, Toys "R" Us, and Wal-Mart. Analysts see better-than-average growth for these companies. Old nifty 50 stocks that aren't on most new lists include Avon Products, Johnson & Johnson, Halliburton, Hewlett-Packard, K-Mart, Polaroid, Procter & Gamble, Schlumberger, and Xerox. A few of the old glamour stocks, such as American Express, AMP, Walt Disney, Digital Equipment, Marriott, and McDonald's, look attractive once again. Such factors as improved management, new products, or the lack of significant competitors are giving these companies new sheen." The continual emergence of new firms and the disappearance of others provides a highly dynamic situation with a wide variation in the attention of analysts. When all of this is combined with the institutional constraints mentioned earlier, the shadows look quite enduring.

Data on shifts in analysts' attention over time confirms the durability of the shadows. Analysis of a sample of 416 companies with ten years of available data in the S&P 500 and a random sample of 403 outside the S&P 500, demonstrated that even relatively well-known companies remain neglected for long periods. Within the S&P 500 sample, 28 percent of the firms originally classified as neglected in 1971 were still classified that way in 1980. Needless to say, the shadow classification is more persistent for lower-profile companies: 82 percent of the non-S&P 500 sample remained neglected for the same ten-year period.

According to the evidence, both statistical and anecdotal, there appears to be little chance that the shadows will suddenly be filled with research floodlights. Informational shadows are an enduring feature of the Wall Street and other investment landscapes. However, mere acceptance of their existence begs the question of their investment potential, which is the topic of the next chapter.

2

SHADOW EFFECTS

Is there any evidence that differences in available information affect returns? How does the investment performance of stocks in the spotlight differ from those in the shadows? This chapter describes the research trail which links contrarian strategies to the shadows. The emphasis is on the more rigorously documented reports of contrarian-type investment anomalies. The evidence is presented in some detail, in order to show how these effects are interrelated and to indicate the level of returns which can be realistically expected in the shadows.

CONTRARIAN EFFECTS

"I just look for disasters, there's nothing I like more than a great disaster. My ears perk up and I get very excited. I think back about things like American Express in the early 1960s, or Rowntree McIntosh, the English company, where cocoa traders were shorting cocoa when they were not supposed to be, and the company nearly went bankrupt. Lockheed is another one, Tampax was one a few years ago with toxic shock. Chrysler you all know about."

The examples cited by James Rogers, co-founder of the Quantum Fund, personify the intuition behind the contrarian approach. In more pithy language, James W. Michaels, the editor of *Forbes* magazine, stated, "Individual investors can achieve superior results by playing against the experts." Although there are many ways of running against the tide of consensus, David Dreman, in *Contrarian Investment Strategy*, argued that the key to success lay in stocks with low price-earnings ratios. In so doing, he tapped the long and rich line of anecdotal and statistical evidence suggesting that the best investment returns were on low price and, especially, low P/E stocks.

The first solid evidence on the P/E ratio, as a statistically reliable measure of subsequent market performance, was provided in 1960. In a follow-up article, Francis Nicholson examined the performance of low versus high P/E stocks, using a sample of 189 high-quality firms in 18 industries over the 25-year period between 1937 and 1962. (See Table 2.1.)

Based on their P/E rankings, the stocks were divided into five equal groups, or quintiles, which were kept intact and then reformed after the periods shown in Table 2.1. The average price appreciation after one year was 16 percent for the lowest P/E quintile versus only 3 percent for the highest P/E group. Even after

TABLE 2.1   Performance of Stocks According to P/E Ranking

P/E Quintile 1937–1962	Average Price Appreciation Percentages after						
	1 yr	2 yr	3 yr	4 yr	5 yr	6 yr	7 yr
1 (Highest)	3%	11%	21%	31%	46%	65%	84%
2	6	14	24	35	50	65	83
3	7	18	30	43	60	77	96
4	9	22	34	48	65	82	100
5 (Lowest)	16	34	55	76	98	125	149

Source: S. Francis Nicholson, "Price-Earnings Ratios," *Financial Analysts Journal,* Jan./Feb. 1968, pp. 105–109. Reprinted with permission.

maintaining the same groups for seven years, the low P/E stocks yielded a return of 149 percent, almost double the performance of the high P/E group with 84 percent.

The big problem with Nicholson's study, as well as those carried out by many others in the following years, was the absence of any adjustment for the possible differences in risk between high and low P/E stocks. This important omission was corrected by Sanjoy Basu in a study of 750 firms from the New York Stock Exchange between 1956 and 1971. As a measure of risk, Basu employed the coefficient of systematic risk relative to the market portfolio, the well-known beta. (More will be said about this and other measures of risk in Chapters 3 and 5. At this point, it is sufficient to note that, despite some problems, beta is still widely accepted as one of the better measures of risk in a portfolio setting.)

The results of Basu's study are shown in Table 2.2. A beta of one implies the same relative risk as the market portfolio; beta greater than one indicates higher risk and beta less than one lower risk. The second column shows the annual returns on the five portfolios constructed by using the P/E ranking at the beginning of the annual measurement period. The third column lists the corresponding portfolio risk coefficients. The striking thing is that not only does the low P/E portfolio have the highest returns, but it also has a lower beta (0.9866) than the beta (1.1121) of the highest P/E quintile. Hence, the contrarian claim that, after risk adjustment, low P/E stocks outperform the market by a wider margin than before risk adjustment. Higher beta is not the reason for the P/E effect.

TABLE 2.2   Systematic Risk and Performance According
to P/E Ranking

P/E Quintile 1957–1971	Average Annual Rate of Return	Beta (Systematic Risk)
A (Highest)	9.3%	1.1121
A*	9.6	1.0579
B	9.3	1.0387
C	11.7	0.9678
D	13.6	0.9401
E (Lowest)	16.3	0.9866

A = highest P/E quintile

A* = highest P/E quintile, excluding stocks with negative earnings.

Source: S. Basu, "Investment Performance of Common Stocks in Relation to Their Price-Earnings Ratios: A Test of the Efficient Market Hypothesis," *Journal of Finance*, June 1977. Reprinted with permission.

SIZE FACTOR

Confirmation of the P/E effect naturally raised questions about the validity of the claim by financial economists that nobody can consistently beat the market averages using publicly available information. So academics took out their research guns and went hunting in droves for the cause. Rolf Banz and Marc Reinganum came up with a possible culprit in the form of company size as expressed by the market value of the firm's equity.

With a sample of NYSE stocks, Banz demonstrated that portfolios of smaller firms had higher returns than portfolios of larger firms, even after making adjustments for risk. The size effect in Banz's sample was not linear; only the very small firms on the NYSE earned superior returns. He concluded, "There is no theoretical foundation for such an effect. We do not even know whether the factor is size itself, or whether size is just a proxy for one or more true but unknown factors correlated with size." Banz did not investigate whether size was merely a proxy variable for the P/E ratio.

This is where Reinganum comes in. He investigated the relationship between the size effect and the P/E effect. For empirical as well as econometric simplicity he looked at the earnings yield, which is the reciprocal of the P/E ratio, rather than the P/E ratio itself. He also expanded on the results of Banz by including securities listed on the American Stock Exchange.

Ten portfolios were formed on the basis of market value in each of the fourteen years of the study, 1963–1977. The daily portfolio returns were then risk-adjusted, to estimate excess returns, by subtracting out the returns from the equally weighted NYSE-AMEX market index. Column one in Table 2.3 lists the ten portfolios formed on the basis of relative market value (MV). Column two reports the mean daily excess returns of the size portfolios. As a measure of the risk of the portfolios relative to the market, column three lists the mean portfolio beta for each of the ten portfolios over the fourteen years of the study. Column four shows the percentage of stocks in each portfolio from the AMEX, and column five reports the average median market value of the stocks in each portfolio.

The results of the study are clear-cut. The low capitalization portfolios earned positive daily excess returns over the sample period, with MV1 earning .05 percent per day and MV2 earning about .02 percent per day, all without incurring any substantial extra market risk: the beta of these two small firm portfolios was only 1.00 and 1.02, respectively. The superior performance of small capitalization stocks is dramatized by the inferior performance of the larger capitalization portfolios. Beginning with portfolio MV5 and

TABLE 2.3   Performance According to Size (Market Value)

Market Value Portfolios 1963–1977	Mean Daily Excess Returns	Beta	Number from AMEX	Average Median Value
MV1 Smallest	.050 %	1.00	82.61 %	$ 8.3 million
MV2	.019	1.02	48.35	20.0
MV3	−.003	1.00	23.81	34.1
MV4	−.005	1.00	11.29	54.5
MV5	−.012	0.94	8.59	86.1
MV6	−.019	0.88	4.42	138.3
MV7	−.019	0.90	4.35	233.5
MV8	−.021	0.83	2.71	413.0
MV9	−.029	0.83	2.46	705.3
MV10 Largest	−.034	0.82	1.60	1759.0

Source: Marc Reinganum, "Misspecification of Capital Asset Pricing: Empirical Anomalies Based on Earnings Yields and Market Values," *Journal of Financial Economics*, Vol. 9, 1981. Reprinted with permission.

continuing through portfolio MV10, each portfolio earned significant negative excess returns ranging from −.01 percent to −.03 percent per day. The difference in returns from MV1 to MV10 was approximately .08 percent per day, which amounts to an impressive return differential on an annual basis.

As one would expect, the smallest market value portfolio was dominated by securities listed on the AMEX; 82.61 percent of portfolio MV1 came from the AMEX. The percentage of AMEX stocks in each portfolio declined across the higher market value portfolios until only 1.6 percent of the stocks found in portfolio MV10 were listed on the AMEX. This might suggest that exchange listing is behind the size effect. However, in Banz's study, where only NYSE stocks were analyzed, the small firm effect still existed, albeit not as strongly. The size effect, apparently, does not depend on the exchange where the stocks are listed.

Reinganum also tested whether the size effect was the result of a P/E effect. He separated the two effects by forming five portfolios of stocks on the basis of the stock's market value and then five subportfolios on the basis of each stock's earnings yield. The findings are shown in Table 2.4.

Reinganum's results suggest that there is no P/E effect when the average size of a firm in the portfolio is held constant. Remembering that low P/E stocks are high E/P stocks, we find that, when size is held constant, the P/E effect disappears. Moving down any of the size columns, there is no relationship between E/P and returns. In other words, the contrarian P/E effect could be said to be an artifact of firm size.

TABLE 2.4   Daily Excess Returns by Size and Earnings Yield

Earnings Yield Quintile 1963–1977	Size (Market Value Quintiles)				
	Smallest 1	2	3	4	Largest 5
1 Lowest	.054%	.0001%	−.009%	−.029%	−.035%
2	.033	−.010	−.031	−.029	−.032
3	.030	−.012	−.022	−.018	−.026
4	.024	−.003	−.012	−.006	−.021
5 Highest	.038	.003	−.001	−.008	−.023

Source: Reinganum, "Misspecification of Capital Asset Pricing," *Journal of Financial Economics*, Vol. 9, 1981. Reprinted with permission.

The procedure can be repeated to determine if there is a size effect after controlling for P/E. This can be examined by selecting any earnings yield (E/P) quintile and studying the portfolio returns across market value quintiles. For example, along the lowest E/P quintile row, we find that the smaller-market-value portfolios outperform the larger-market-value portfolios. The same is true within any of the E/P rows. These results imply that the size effect exists even after controlling for the P/E ratio. Investing against the market consensus seems to be a matter of selecting small firms rather than large ones.

This finding hardly satisfied the academic researchers, because there is no fundamental reason why small-firm stocks should outperform the market any more than low P/E stocks. The chase for an explanation had to continue.

THE JANUARY PHENOMENON

Shortly after the unveiling of the enigmatic size effect, Donald Keim published evidence that size was strongly related to yet another anomaly, which he baptized as the "January effect." He demonstrated that fully one half of the abnormal returns ascribed to the size effect can be shown to occur during the month of January. Furthermore, half of the January effect occurs during the first five trading days of the month. A phenomenal January effect occurred in 1987, with the Dow (and other markets) hitting all time highs.

Clearly, something about the month of January is impinging on the stock market to produce abnormally high returns for small firms. Since the size effect is approximately 20 percent per year after risk adjustment, Keim's results imply that abnormal returns of 10 percent occur during the month of January and excess returns of 5 percent could be earned during the first trading week in January alone.

Initially, tax-loss selling at the end of the calendar year, followed by a subsequent price rebound at the beginning of the next year, was thought to provide a reasonable explanation of this phenomenon. Recently, however, Brown, Keim, Kleindon, and Marsh have questioned this explanation of the January effect. The Australian stock market, where the tax year ends on June 30, exhibits not only a size effect, but also a January effect, plus a June tax loss selling effect. Since a January effect exists in the Australian market with a different tax cycle, tax-loss selling alone is probably not the only cause of the January effect in the U.S. markets.

Needless to say, the failure of tax loss selling as an explanation of the January phenomenon did little to clarify the economics behind the size effect; if anything, it complicated the issue. Not only did the size effect remain unexplained, but there was the added need for an explanation of why the superior returns were concentrated in January.

ANALYSTS' NEGLECT

Signs of a possible breakthrough in the puzzle came with the presentation of evidence by Arbel and Strebel suggesting a link between the size effect and the availability of information. They showed that highly researched stocks are outperformed by those that analysts neglect and that size and neglect are linked.

The number of professional security analysts following the firm was employed as a measure of the intensity of the informational shadows. Professional analysts are experts at shifting through large quantities of data, interpreting the data's impact on a company's operations, and reporting their findings, so that investors will understand the implications of this information for the value of the company's stock. This process differentiates the level of information available on companies in the market. The true difference lies in the amount of information, not data, which is available on the possible future course of a company. Analysts provide the critical link between the company's data and information which has investment value (see Chapter 1).

Analysts look for and interpret data in different ways. Sometimes one analyst will not see a factor that can mean the difference between success and failure, or profit and loss. There is a lower likelihood of two or three analysts' missing something, than for one analyst to do so. Likewise, the possibility of ten or more analysts all missing an important factor is very low. In general, the more analysts who study a stock, the higher the level of information available on the stock.

Using the Standard and Poor's Earnings Forecaster to identify the level of analysts' attention for the S&P 500, Arbel and Strebel classified stocks into three groups based on each stock's level of analyst coverage. The group with the highest relative level of analyst coverage was called Research Concentration Ranking One (RCR 1), and the portfolio of the least researched companies, Research Concentration Ranking Three (RCR 3). The results of the study, encompassing the period 1972–1976, are presented in Table 2.5 below.

Table 2.5 shows the performance of the three portfolios in each of the five years and over the whole five-year period. The first column of findings reports the annual returns for each portfolio. Every year the return from the portfolio neglected by research analysts outperformed the highly researched portfolio: The latter portfolio (RCR 1) earned an average of only 6.6 percent per year, compared

TABLE 2.5   Performance by Category of Analysts' Neglect

Year	Research Concentration Ranking (RCR)	Annual Return	Annual Excess Return
1972	RCR 1 Followed	18.3%	0.5%
	RCR 2	12.5	6.2
	RCR 3 Neglected	18.9	1.4
1973	RCR 1 Followed	20.6	3.7
	RCR 2	22.1	4.5
	RCR 3 Neglected	9.7	7.8
1974	RCR 1 Followed	28.2	3.4
	RCR 2	25.5	7.9
	RCR 3 Neglected	12.3	17.8
1975	RCR 1 Followed	40.5	3.7
	RCR 2	51.1	13.4
	RCR 3 Neglected	54.1	16.3
1976	RCR 1 Followed	23.1	4.5
	RCR 2	33.2	13.6
	RCR 3 Neglected	37.3	19.8
Average 1972–1976	RCR 1 Followed	6.6	1.7
	RCR 2	9.8	4.8
	RCR 3 Neglected	17.7	12.6

Source: Avner Arbel and Paul Strebel, "The Neglected and Small Firm Effects." *The Financial Review*, November, 1982. Reprinted with permission.

to the neglected portfolio in the shadows (RCR 3), which earned 17.7 percent.

Column two of findings in Table 2.5 lists the average excess returns of the portfolios during the sample period. The risk-adjusted excess portfolio returns in column three confirm and enhance the results obtained before risk adjustment. During each of the five years, the neglected portfolio earned substantially higher excess returns than the highly researched portfolio. Over the entire five-year period, the neglected portfolio (RCR 3) yielded an average annual excess return of 12.6 percent compared to an insignificant 1.7 percent excess return for the highly researched portfolio (RCR 1).

The superior returns on neglected stocks raise the question of the possible interplay between neglect and size. One would expect a strong correlation between analysts' neglect and market value. The activities of professional security analysts are motivated by the desire to sell their research. Since the demand for information is a function of the number of current and potential shareholders, the larger-capitalization firms tend to have more shareholders and hence a higher demand for information. Analysts provide this information until the point where it becomes unprofitable to do so, which is reached much sooner for small-capitalization companies.

Contrary to popular belief, not all highly researched stocks have large market values. Similarly, neglected stocks are not all small. Table 2.6 shows the distribution of market value size within each of the research concentration rankings (RCR). Most of the highly researched stocks in RCR 1 are also large-capitalization companies. However, upon examination of the first row in Table 2.6, it is evident that only 54 percent of the stocks in RCR 1 belong to the top three market value categories. Likewise, most of the stocks in the neglected sector of the market are also small-capitalization stocks. Yet only 55 percent of all stocks in the neglected portfolio (RCR 3) are in the three smallest market value categories.

Arbel and Strebel found that both size and neglect had an impact on returns, but that neither was dominant. However, the study was limited in several ways. First, the measurement period covered only five years. Second, the sample was restricted to the S&P 500. Third, and possibly most important, analysts' attention was measured by the number of analysts forecasting earnings per share in the Standard and Poor's Earnings forecaster. The S&P Earnings

TABLE 2.6 Percentage Distribution by Size and Neglect (Research Concentration)

Research Concentration Ranking 1976	Size Deciles									
	Smallest 1	2	3	4	5	6	7	8	9	Largest 10
RCR 1 Followed	0.7%	6.1%	4.1%	6.8%	8.7%	7.4%	12.2%	10.1%	19.6%	24.3%
RCR 2	8.2	11.7	12.2	10.7	11.2	13.3	11.7	11.7	6.1	3.2
RCR 3 Neglected	27.9	12.4	15.0	14.0	9.7	6.5	3.7	6.5	3.2	1.1

Source: Avner Arbel and Paul Strebel, "The Neglected and Small Firm Effects," *The Financial Review*, November, 1982. Reprinted with permission.

Forecaster canvasses only about 50 analysts to obtain a consensus measure of earnings per share. Yet there are well over one thousand analysts who produce these earnings per share estimates on a timely basis. The S&P Forecaster represents only a small fraction, less than 5 percent of the total population of analysts in the market.

INSTITUTIONAL NEGLECT

Institutional holdings, easier to obtain at the time than analysts' attention, provide an interesting alternative measure of neglect. The involvement of institutions in the stock market is substantial. Institutions own nearly 75 percent of the total market value of stocks listed on the NYSE. According to the *Wall Street Journal*, they account for 80 to 90 percent of the total dollar trading volume on an average day. In some ways, institutions are model investors: They typically purchase enough stocks from different industries and sectors to completely diversify their portfolios. They also engage numerous money managers and research analysts to monitor their massive holdings on a continuous basis. The resulting proliferation of information dissemination on stocks widely held by institutions causes an information asymmetry to occur. Stocks owned by many institutional investors have relatively more information available concerning a wider scope of possible future events than stocks of institutionally neglected companies.

Early evidence of investment performance premiums on institutionally neglected firms was presented by W. Scott Bauman. In 1964, he reported that stocks held by only one or two investment companies outperformed a group of widely held stocks. The performance differential was shown to exist for most of the ten-year period from 1954 through 1963. According to a recent (1986) Morgan Stanley report, "The proverbial 'little guy' obviously knew something to outperform his institutional brethren for eight years. The performance of institutionally overowned stocks relative to institutionally underowned issues is embarrassing. You would make money if you simply bought every stock the learned institutions sold."

More recent evidence of the performance premiums offered by institutionally neglected firms was documented by Arbel, Carvell, and Strebel. The level of institutional coverage for each company was measured by the number of institutions holding a particular stock as reported in the Standard and Poor's Monthly Stock Guide over the ten-year period from 1971–1981 in a sample of over 500 companies.

The first part of the study was designed to show that there is an institutional neglected firm effect, such that stocks neglected by institutions exhibit higher returns than those normally predicted by the stock's level of systematic risk. Repeating the design of the previous study based on analysts' attention, this study separated the stocks first into three different portfolios based on the level of institutional holdings. Institutional Concentration Ranking One (ICR 1) contained stocks owned by more than 12 institutions. ICR 2 contained those stocks with between two and twelve institutions holding shares, and ICR 3, stocks with zero or one institutional holding.

The first column of results in Table 2.7 shows the total returns on the three ICR portfolios. There is evidence here of a strong neglected firm effect. Stocks that were institutionally neglected earned almost double the returns of those stocks that were widely held. The neglected portfolio (ICR 3) yielded 20.84 percent per year compared to a 10.36 percent annual return for the highly researched portfolio (ICR 1). This represents a ten percent return premium on the neglected stocks in the shadows.

The return differential exists even after risk adjustment. Column two shows the excess returns, after adjustment for market-related systematic risk, for the three ICR portfolios. The neglected portfolio (ICR 3) generated 5.64 percent in excess returns per year compared to a −5.8 percent in excess returns for the institutional favorites. The excess return differential is still over 10 percent.

Yet once again the size factor raises its head. Institutions are

TABLE 2.7   Performance by Category of Institutional Neglect

Institutional Concentration Ranking 1971–1980	Average Annual Return	Annual Excess Return
ICR 1: Intensively held	10.36%	−5.80%
ICR 2: Moderately held	16.89	1.11
ICR 3: Institutionally neglected	20.84	5.64

Source: Arbel, Carvell, and Strebel, "Giraffes, Institutions and Neglected Firms," Financial Analysts Journal, May/June 1983, pp. 2–8. Reprinted with permission.

constrained in their investing for several reasons, all related to the same factor: firm size. Institutions typically own less than 5 percent of a company's stock to avoid filing insider trading reports. This places a purchase ceiling on the institution's holdings. As the market value of a company's common stock drops, so does the investment position of the institution. Institutions also avoid taking very small positions in many different stocks because of the tremendous monitoring costs associated with such a strategy. Furthermore, because institutions typically trade in multiple blocks, they do not invest in companies with floats insufficient to handle large block trading without adverse price effects. Finally, because of fiduciary requirements, institutions are, for the most part, bound to follow the prudent man model. Invest in the "tried and true" and no one can question—or litigate—your judgment.

The combination of these factors causes a form of market tiering, which brings size to the fore, as possibly the dominant effect in the shadows. Owing to the constraints which prevent institutions from participating strongly in the lower tier, the smaller-capitalization companies are required to earn higher returns for their noninstitutional shareholders. Furthermore, because the constraints on institutional investors are not likely to disappear, neither is the tiering. Thus, permanent tiering directly related to market capitalization and institutional investors' practices may be the overriding cause of the neglected firm effect.

To determine whether size or institutional neglect per se is dominant, the two effects were evaluated at the same time, as shown in Table 2.8. First, the stocks were broken into three portfolios based on institutional neglect and then into three portfolios based on market value. Returns and excess returns were then calculated for the resulting nine portfolios.

The results are interesting. Although size and institutional neglect are highly correlated, the pattern of relative dominance is indisputable. Moving across any row, we see that larger firms actually earn higher returns than smaller firms. In other words, after controlling for institutional neglect, there is no size effect. However, the neglected firm effect is pervasive throughout all size groups. Moving down any column, we see that the more neglected firms always earn higher returns. The neglected firm effect still exists after controlling for firm size.

The results are reinforced after controlling for systematic mar-

TABLE 2.8   Annual Returns by Size and Institutional Neglect

Institutional Concentration Ranking 1971–1980	Size		
	Small 1	2	Large 3
ICR 1: Intensively held	N/A	0.086%	0.109%
ICR 2: Moderately held	0.147	0.173	0.232
ICR 3: Institutionally neglected	0.201	0.260	N/A

N/A: not available owing to insufficient data.

Source: Arbel, Carvell, and Strebel, "Giraffes, Institutions and Neglected Firms," *Financial Analysts Journal*, May/June 1983, pp. 2–8. Reprinted with permission.

ket risk. The pattern of excess returns is the same as the pattern of total returns. The neglected firm effect persists after controlling for firm size, whereas the small firm effect disappears after controlling for institutional neglect. Thus, the return premiums on small firms seem to be a function of the lack of information in the shadows as captured by institutional neglect.

LISTING PERIOD

The idea that the small firm effect might be due to differences in available information was reinforced by Christopher Barry and Stephen Brown. They used the length of time a stock has been publicly listed to measure available information, because the longer a stock has been listed, the greater should be the information network surrounding it. The listing period variable had the important advantage of allowing Barry and Brown to test the information hypothesis over a 50-year period from 1931 to 1980.

For each month, a sample of NYSE securities was classified into categories based on the previous month's market value and the number of months since the security was first listed. The portfolios were separated into six categories based on firm size and period of listing. Table 2.9 presents the risk-adjusted performance of the 36 portfolios formed on the basis of listing period. Portfolio one represents those stocks listed for a relatively short period of time, about 89.5 months on average. Portfolio six, on the other hand, is com-

TABLE 2.9   Monthly Excess Returns by Size and Period of Listing

		Period of Listing					
		Shortest 1	2	3	4	5	Longest 6
Smallest	1	2.60%	2.03%	2.19%	0.52%	0.94%	0.68%
	2	1.71	1.99	0.42	−0.64	−0.71	−0.84
	3	−0.26	0.28	1.18	−3.13	−0.56	−0.26
	4	−0.82	−1.44	−1.03	−0.45	−1.11	−0.90
	5	0.55	−1.42	−0.18	0.53	0.21	−.236
Largest	6	−1.83	−2.25	−2.37	−1.55	−2.81	−2.85
Period of Listing Portfolios		2.20%	1.21%	1.76%	−1.24%	−1.79%	−1.70%

Source: Christopher Barry and Stephen Brown, "Differential Information and the Small Firm Effect," *Journal of Financial Economics*, Vol. 13, 1984. Reprinted with permission.

posed of those stocks listed for the longest period of time, 592.1 months on average.

A strong listing effect is present in the bottom row of data. The short listing period portfolio (portfolio 1) earned an average monthly excess return of 2.2 percent per month compared to −1.7 percent for the longer listed portfolio (portfolio 6).

Does the listing effect still exist after controls are made for size? Moving across the rows, the results show that the listing effect is strongest for the smaller market value portfolios (portfolios 1 and 2). The size effect is also apparent in the data. Move down any of the columns: as the average market value increases, the monthly excess returns decline. However, the size effect is much stronger for stocks listed for a shorter period of time, (see column 1). The evidence in Table 2.9 indicates that neither size nor period of listing dominates.

Why doesn't the period of listing, which is a shadows variable, dominate size in the same way as institutional neglect? Apparently, the period of listing is not as good an indicator of information availability as institutional neglect. Its performance in capturing the size effect is comparable to that of the S&P Earnings Forecaster measure of analysts' attention. This is not surprising, because the period of listing is a static variable in that a company will always have the same listing date, regardless of how famous it becomes. Nevertheless, taken overall, the period of listing data confirms the existence of superior returns in the shadows.

A SINGLE SHADOW EFFECT

The research described so far constitutes a trail which seems to lead from contrarian strategies directly into the shadows. The contrarian P/E effect is apparently dominated by the size effect. The latter, in turn, seems to be dominated by variables measuring the availability of information, especially institutional neglect. On the other hand, the ambiguous performance of the S&P Forecaster and Listing Period variables, as explanatory factors of the size effect, raises the question of whether another informational or neglect indicator might be available to remove any nagging doubt about the role of the shadows.

Fortunately, a much better source of analysts' attention than the S&P Forecaster is available in the form of the Institutional Brokers Estimate System (I/B/E/S) produced by Lynch, Jones, and Ryan, Inc. I/B/E/S started publishing consensus estimates in 1976; they canvass over 1200 analysts for their earnings forecasts. The data base provides the most complete source of the number of analysts following a company and their earnings.

Carvell and Strebel used I/B/E/S to test the robustness of analysts' neglect as a key shadows variable. For the period from 1976 to 1981, a random sample of 865 stocks was separated into three groups for each month of the study. This time, stocks with more than nine analysts were considered highly researched and placed in portfolio one (RCR 1). Stocks with between three and eight analysts were regarded as moderately researched (RCR 2). Stocks with less than three analysts were taken as neglected and placed in RCR 3.

The interaction between size and analysts' neglect is displayed in Table 2.10 for the nine portfolios obtained by dividing each of the RCR portfolios into three size portfolios based on market value. The important point is that the neglected firm effect, based on the IBES measure of analysts' attention, now dominates the small firm

TABLE 2.10   Monthly Returns by Size and Analysts' Neglect

		Size		
Research Concentration		Small		Large
Ranking 1976–1981		1	2	3
RCR 1	Returns	−1.6%	1.1%	1.1%
Closely followed	Excess returns	−2.5	0.2	−.09
RCR 2	Returns	1.1	1.8	1.7
	Excess returns	−0.4	0.4	0.5
RCR 3	Returns	2.4	2.3	2.4
Neglected	Excess returns	1.1	1.2	1.3

Source: Steven Carvell and Paul Strebel, "Is There a Neglected Firm Effect?," *Journal of Business Finance and Accounting,* Forthcoming 1987. Reprinted with permission.

effect. Moving across any of the RCR portfolios, we see that portfolio returns typically increase as market value increases, that is, a reverse size effect. This effect is strongest in RCR 1 and RCR 2. By contrast, the neglected firm effect prevails regardless of the market value category. Moving down any size classification, we see that portfolio returns rise as the level of neglect increases. Specifically, in the medium-sized portfolio (2), returns go from 1.1 percent per month for highly researched stocks to 2.3 percent per month for the neglected stocks.

The claim that the size effect is dominated by the neglected firm effect is reinforced by the pattern of risk-adjusted excess returns. Without exception, within any RCR group, as we move from small to large capitalization stocks, the excess returns do not decrease, as the small firm effect would predict, but increase. As before, the size effect is apparently reversed after controlling for the level of analysts' neglect; the larger capitalization stocks earn higher excess returns. By contrast, the neglected firm effect is everywhere apparent after controlling for market value. Moving down any of the size categories, we find that excess returns rise with the more neglected stocks. Thus, when a more sophisticated data source is used, the apparent contradiction between the investment performance of analysts' and institutional neglect is eliminated.

Vanishing Shadows?

A question often posed about market abnormalities asks, if the market acts efficiently won't the abnormality disappear? In Chapter 3 we explain conceptually why the answer is "unlikely" when asked of stocks in the shadows. However, conceptual discourse is no substitute for empirical evidence. The results of a recent study by Arbel and Carvell provide such evidence. They enhanced and updated the results of Table 2.10 concentrating on the performance of NYSE stocks during the five year period between January 1981 and December 1985. The only major difference is that they formed portfolios into five groups based on size and neglect instead of three.

As it turned out, this time period proved especially interesting. Evidence indicates that, over the five year period from 1981–1985, the size effect was *reversed*. In other words, for the NYSE as a whole, larger capitalization firms earned higher returns than did smaller capitalization firms. Proof of this reversed size effect is evident in Table 2.11

Moving along the bottom of the table we find that annual compounded returns go from 25.2 percent for the largest capitalization portfolio down to 10.6 percent for the smallest capitalization portfolio. Large capitalization firms earned an average 15 percent higher per year than small capitalization firms. Although these results are not risk adjusted, few would argue that large firms are *more* risky, so why the reversed size effect? One possible explanation points to business cycles, changes in inflationary expectations, and the relative interest rate sensitivity of small and large capitalization stocks. Another more technical argument suggests that the larger cap "blue chips" were due for a strong price correction and this correction swamped the typically stellar performance of small cap stocks. Whatever the source, the size effect was reversed. So what about the neglected firm effect?

It's still there. Moving down the last column we find evidence that there was a neglected firm effect, albeit weaker than usual, even though the size effect was reversed. The average annual compounded returns of highly researched stocks were only 17.3 percent compared to 25.7 percent for stocks in the shadows. The fact that the neglected firm effect operates independently of the small firm effect supports the notion of a single shadow effect. Whatever drove

**TABLE 2.11 Annual Compound Returns by Size
and Analysts Neglect
1981–1985**

| | | Size | | | | | Average Within Neglect Category |
| | | Small | | Medium | | Large | |
		5	4	3	2	1	
Spotlight	RCR 1	−48.9%	−47.7%	0.9%	11.2%	23.0%	17.3%
	RCR 2	−32.7	−5.1	13.3	24.7	30.1	18.9
	RCR 3	−4.9	15.2	26.5	34.4	28.2	21.6
	RCR 4	6.6	27.2	40.7	36.2	28.9	21.6
Shadows	RCR 5	19.5	38.1	38.9	45.5	46.3	25.7
Average Within Size Group		10.6	21.1	24.0	23.3	25.2	

Source: A. Arbel and S. Carvell, "The Pervasive Neglected Firm Effect," Working Paper, Cornell University, 1987.

the market to correct the "blue chips" at the expense the small caps over this period had only a moderating effect on the neglected firm effect.

In fact, the only reason why the neglected firm effect seems slightly weaker than usual is that we have yet to isolate the impact of a reversed size effect. The first five columns in Table 2.11 each contain stocks of similar market value: 5 (the smallest) to 1 (the largest). Within all size groups, stocks in the shadows outperform those in the spotlight. Moving down any column we find a strong neglected firm effect. Even among medium to very large capitalization stocks, which performed well over this period, stocks in the shadows earned higher returns than those in the spotlight.

As was the case in studies discussed earlier, the size effect continues to be reversed whenever we hold the level of analyst attention constant. Moving across any row we find that large capitalization stocks outperform small ones whether they are in the spotlight (RCR 1) or in the shadows (RCR 5). The consistent existence of a neglected firm effect, regardless of the small firm effect's direction, establishes that the neglected firm effect is independent of any so-called small firm effect. Any anomalous returns normally ascribed to small capitalization companies are therefore attributable to a single shadow effect best measured by a stock's level of relative neglect.

Of course at times small capitalization stocks are in favor and at other times investors prefer the "blue chips." In turn, we expect to find years where there is a normal size effect and years where it is reversed. Regardless of which situation occurs, however, stocks in the shadows will continue to outperform those in the spotlight. The lesson is clear: For both small and large cap stocks, the returns are greatest in the shadows.

Not a January Effect

One final hurdle remains, however, in order to show the absolute dominance of the neglected firm effect over the size effect. Is neglect perhaps related to the January phenomenon? Does the neglected firm effect exist after controlling for the huge returns afforded small-capitalization (and perhaps neglected) stocks during the month of January? To determine this, the analysis was repeated after excluding January's returns from the data.

The portfolio returns and excess returns without the inclusion of January's data are shown in Table 2.12. The results further reinforce the notion that the neglected firm effect is dominant. Without exception, down any size category, the returns and excess returns increase as the level of analysts' neglect increases. The size effect is reversed, however, everywhere except in RCR 2, where excess returns rise slightly with declining market value. The fact that the neglected firm effect exists, regardless of whether or not January's returns are included in the calculation of portfolio returns, indicates that the neglected firm effect is not a by-product of the January phenomenon.

The finding that firm size is merely a proxy for neglect in the shadows was checked by means of two more rigorous tests: first, a two-way factor analysis of the mean excess returns and second, a pooled cross-sectional regression of portfolio returns against beta, number of analysts, and the log of firm size. Both tests, with and without January returns, confirmed the unequivocal statistical dominance of neglect over size.

Is it possible, in addition, that the January phenomenon is somehow also a shadow effect? A comparison of Tables 2.10 and

TABLE 2.12   Monthly Returns by Size and Analysts' Neglect Excluding January

Research Concentration Ranking 1976–1981		Small 1	Size 2	Large 3
RCR 1	Returns	−1.8%	1.0%	1.1%
Closely followed	Excess returns	−2.3	−3.3	0.09
RCR 2	Returns	0.6	1.6	1.7
	Excess returns	0.7	0.3	0.5
RCR 3	Returns	1.8	2.0	2.1
Neglected	Excess returns	0.5	0.9	1.0

Source: Steven Carvell and Paul Strebel, "Is There a Neglected Firm Effect?," *Journal of Business Finance and Accounting*, Forthcoming 1987. Reprinted with permission.

2.11 shows that the inclusion of January returns has the biggest impact in the shadow portfolio (RCR 3). The excess returns on the small neglected portfolio more than double when January returns are included, from 0.5 percent to 1.1 percent per month, while the returns on the large neglected portfolio increase less than a third from 1.0 percent to 1.3 percent per month.

One possible implication of this finding is that part of the January phenomenon, not due to tax loss selling, can be attributed to informational differences between small and large firms at the end of the year. Annual reports, performance reports of investment houses, and numerous investment magazine publications abound at that time of the year. All of this information partially fills the informational vacuum which typically surrounds smaller capitalization firms. The lower level of uncertainty makes these smaller stocks attractive to investors at the turn of the year, forcing up prices, thereby creating the January effect. Some preliminary evidence supporting this hypothesis has been provided by Arbel, who showed that the uncertainty surrounding neglected stocks, as measured by the variance in analysts' earnings forecasts, is at its low point for the year in January. Thus, at least some of the January phenomenon may be attributable to information availability.

In summary, the research described in this chapter suggests that the contrarian P/E effect is really a size effect, that the size effect is really a neglected firm effect, and that the January phenomenon is possibly also a function of information differences. All these anomalies are largely a single shadow effect characterized by a lack of investment information. The effect seems to be best accounted for statistically by variables most closely related to the activity of security analysts. The cumulative sum of the evidence leaves virtually no doubt that, after the standard market risk adjustment procedure, stocks in the spotlight are outperformed by those in the shadows.

3

DISCOUNTS: APPARENT OR REAL?

Does the superior performance of neglected firms mean that investors are automatically better off in the shadows, despite the lack of information? Are the discounts associated with neglected stocks merely apparent, in that they offset the lack of information in the shadows, or do they provide a real opportunity for beating the market averages? In addressing these questions, this chapter describes three dangers which have to be faced by shadow investors and then explores the role of security research in reducing these risks.

INFORMATION EVENTS VS NATURAL EVENTS

The problem with shadow investment is that you cannot see exactly what you are buying. What investors perceive about a shadow stock may be quite different from what is actually happening to the company itself. It is critical to distinguish between natural events affecting the company and information events affecting the market—in the words of Aswath Damodaran, " . . . events generated by nature and the process by which information on these natural events is disseminated to the market." Natural events are those that change the "true" value of the firm, like earthquakes, new product sales, or management decisions changing the firm's operations. Information events change the market value of the firm without affecting "true" value. Some information events reflect natural events, such as earnings announcements, whereas others reflect perceived changes in value by investors, such as a block trade by insiders.

The key point is that the market prices embody only what investors perceive. They do not actually respond to natural events, but to information about these events. In the information spotlight this distinction is not important, because all natural events are rapidly diagnosed by analysts and embodied in coincident information dissemination. Under these conditions, prices reflect natural events, and market value equals true value. In the shadows, however the lack of information may distort the value of the firm. Prices reflect information events, and market value may not always equal true value.

How does the potential shadow distortion of the firm's true value affect investors? It clearly introduces an element of danger or additional risk into the investment decision. Flaws in information can radically alter the shape of a stock's return distribution and, hence, can affect how investors perceive risk in the shadows.

Whether investors are better off in the shadows despite this fact depends on whether the superior returns on neglected firms more than compensate for the extra risk. In analytical terms, the question is whether the typical market risk adjustment, originally developed for the spotlight, is adequate in the shadows.

In Chapter 2, we used the market risk coefficient, beta, without much comment to calculate risk-adjusted excess returns in the shadows as well as in the spotlight. But beta may not be an adequate risk measure in the shadows. More specifically, does beta capture the shadow distortion of the firm's value? To get an answer, it will first be helpful to go back and briefly review some of the well-known principles of investment risk, to see where beta fits in, before proceeding to the more unique dangers of investment in the shadows.

INVESTMENT RISK IN THE SPOTLIGHT

Intuitively, most people identify risk with the possibility of a loss, the chance of a net return on the investment below zero. However, the possibility of negative returns masks the interplay of two dimensions, which are often best looked at separately: the most likely, or average, outcome on the one hand, and the variability in the outcome on the other. An unstable high-tech stock may have the same expected return as a stable blue chip, but the former will have a higher risk of loss. At the company level, moreover, risk of loss is usually associated with the chance of bankruptcy. This masks an additional third dimension, the ability of the company to absorb losses, which depends on the firm's reserves of liquid assets.

The simplest way of avoiding confusion is to define investment risk in terms of the variability in return—more precisely, the chances that the return will be in various ranges around the anticipated average. To the extent that the possible returns are normally distributed, a single statistic, the standard deviation, can be used to describe the volatility in the returns. The standard deviation corresponds to the most likely range of variability around the average, or mean return.

Yet the risk to which a stock exposes an investor may be less than the full return variability. It depends on what else is in the investor's portfolio. At least part of the stock's return variability will be offset by the counter-variability of other stocks in the portfolio. The price fluctuations of a high-tech stock may be partially offset, for example, by the fluctuations in a construction stock. This is the well-known *diversification effect*. The key to the effect is the fact that some of the movement in a firm's share price is caused by factors which are specific to the firm, such as a change in management, loss of a critical customer, or an improvement in efficiency. From the point of view of an investment portfolio, such firm-specific events occur in a random pattern over time. When one firm benefits, another might suffer. Consequently, the sum of these random events across many firms results in little or no change in the total portfolio return.

The remaining portfolio risk is the residual variability in its return. It reflects the individual stock price movements which do not cancel out, that is, the stock price movements which are correlated. In well-diversified portfolios, most of the industry and company specific fluctuations cancel out. The remaining correlations reflect a common dependency on underlying macro-economic factors such as interest rates, the gross national product, or inflation. The corresponding return fluctuations are known as systematic risk, because they occur more or less simultaneously, system-wide, throughout the economy. Beta is the statistical measure of systematic risk.

In the stock market, this type of risk is critical, because it determines how stocks are priced. The assumption is that investors of any consequence in the market are well diversified; that is, they have at least twenty stocks from a wide variety of industries in their portfolio. For a given company, the only risk that matters to these investors is the systematic part, induced by the economy-wide factors. The rest of the stock's return fluctuations, due to industry and company-specific factors, the unsystematic risk, cancels out and does not come into the pricing decision. As a result, the value of the security is based on its perceived systematic risk only.

In the shadows, however, the estimation of systematic risk can be quite tricky, owing to the influence of a number of special conditions to which we now turn.

SHADOW DANGER ONE: ESTIMATION RISK

The basic lack of information in the shadows makes it difficult to assess the parameters of a stock's return distribution. The lack of information results in many more errors in analysts' forecasts of the company's prospects and their estimates of the parameters of the return distribution. Specifically, the poor information results in uncertainty about the exact position of the return distribution, the estimates of the mean, standard deviation, and correlation with economy-wide factors. This kind of uncertainty is called *estimation risk*.

Historical estimates of systematic risk, in particular, tend to be much less reliable in the shadows than in the spotlight. Firms in the shadows may not have been listed long enough to generate sufficient data for the reliable estimation of systematic risk. Moreover, neglected firms often have much less well-diversified business portfolios, because they are generally smaller than companies in the spotlight. The lack of business diversification increases their unsystematic risk, which in turn increases the likelihood of an error associated with the measurement of systematic risk.

In addition, the scarcity of analysts' information about the company's future decreases the chances for sharpening the historical risk estimate. Analysts' reports provide frequent information concerning the probable impact of environmental changes on the stock of the company. Their reports typically carry an analysis of the industry's prospects in the context of the evolving economic scene, together with an assessment of the company's competitive standing within that industry. For example, an anticipated change in the level of interest rates and its likely impact on stocks in the forestry, construction, real estate, and banking industries may imply substantial revisions in historically derived systematic risk coefficients. None of this is available in the deep shadows, where investors have to make do with unreliable historical estimates of risk, without the benefit of forward-looking analysts' research.

The net result is many more estimation errors in the shadows than in the spotlight. Forced to trade in the dark, shadow investors are frequently wide of the mark. When a clearer view of the events is revealed over time, investors are forced to correct their valuation estimates. The pricing corrections generated by estimation errors show up in larger return fluctuations. This causes the return distributions in the shadows to have wider spreads than in the spotlight. Hence, estimation errors increase the width of shadow return distributions.

Diversifiable Nature of Estimation Risk

Fortunately, for well-diversified investors, estimation risk is essentially offsetting and unsystematic. Estimation errors are no more likely to be positive than negative. No obvious reason exists why investors should systematically under- or overestimate the value of stocks in the shadows. Indeed, if estimation errors were biased in either direction, this would show up in the subsequent pricing behavior of the stock concerned. Being rational, the average investor would immediately compensate for any estimation bias that might exist. Intuition, therefore, strongly suggests that the additional estimation risk in the shadow can be diversified away.

Some observers argue, however, that the typical investor is not that well-diversified. Since larger financial institutions are often precluded from investing in the smaller neglected stocks, investors who make up the market for most neglected stocks might be smaller and less well-diversified. If so, proportionately less of the total risk in the shadows would be diversified away and more would be perceived to be systematic, thereby lowering the price and raising the return on neglected stocks. Unfortunately, it is very difficult to get information on portfolio compositions, especially for shadow investors, so that this hypothesis cannot readily be tested. Moreover, the argument is not very convincing, because it implies a form of market segmentation that is difficult to reconcile with the increasing integration and frequency of arbitrage throughout the financial markets.

The potential role of estimation risk in the pricing of capital assets has been the subject of whole series of articles which appeared in the finance literature during the late nineteen-seventies and early nineteen-eighties. A dominant view which emerged was that estimation risk is indeed irrelevant in the sense that it is diversified and, hence, doesn't affect the pricing decision. Thus, Bawa and Brown concluded, "In empirical testing of equilibrium pricing, one should not necessarily be concerned with the problem of estimation risk or expect estimation risk to be a factor explaining any possible deviations between the theory and observed market rates of return." No viable argument can be based on the notion of systematic estimation errors which investors refuse to correct. Estimation risk per se, despite important practical implications to be discussed later on, probably has nothing to do with the explanation of the shadow effect.

Figure 3.1 illustrates the relationship between future estimation risk and the historically observed neglected firm effect. The vertical axis measures returns, while the horizontal axis measures systematic risk. The diagonal line depicts the current risk-return tradeoff. The typical followed stock with return $R_{followed}$ and systematic risk β_F lies on the tradeoff line. The typical neglected stock with return $R_{neglected}$ and systematic risk β_N lies above the line. The vertical distance above the line reflects the superior returns on neglected firms discussed in Chapter 2, that is, the historically observed neglected firm effect.

The circles around the positions of the neglected and followed stocks represent the corresponding levels of estimation risk. The larger circle around the neglected stock illustrates the much greater

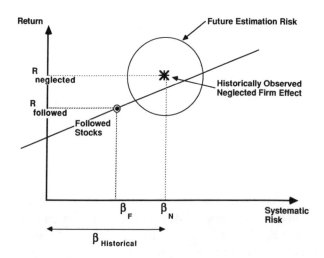

Figure 3.1   Future estimation risk and the historically observed neglected firm effect.

errors involved in estimating future risk and return in the shadows relative to the spotlight. The fact that the circles are centered on the positions of the stocks reflects the absence of bias associated with estimation risk. The estimation risk circle surrounding the neglected stock can be tightened through diversification (see Chapter 5). However, as shown by the findings in Chapter 2, diversification cannot explain the superior returns on neglected firms, in that it does not move the neglected stock portfolio onto the tradeoff line.

SHADOW DANGER TWO: EXTRAPOLATION RISK

The infrequent release of information obscures the intrinsic fluctuations in the performance of neglected firms. Earnings and other changes are revealed to investors only from time to time. When information arrives, it reflects the impact of all natural events since the last piece of information. The corresponding returns capture more information, so they tend to be much higher, or lower, than the true return. Figure 3.2 illustrates the typical pattern of returns in the shadows. Returns are plotted on the vertical axis and time on the horizontal axis. The release of positive information results

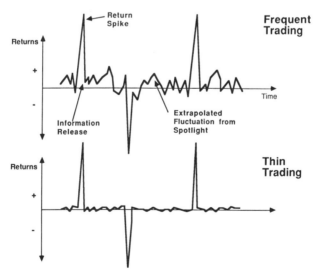

Figure 3.2   Return spikes and extrapolation risk in the shadows.

in positive return spikes, while negative information causes negative spikes.

Between the periodic information disclosure and the corresponding return spikes, investors are forced to extrapolate information from the spotlight into the shadows. The impact of environmental change on the value of neglected firms might be assessed by comparison with comparable companies that are more heavily researched. In the case of a neglected computer company, for example, the effect of shifting demand patterns in the computer industry could be extrapolated from the research generated about a computer company in the spotlight. Events of this nature are common whenever IBM's earnings are adjusted by analysts. Such information from the spotlight will be used, because without it the valuation of the firm would reflect only part of the available information set.

Impact of Trading Frequency

With respect to the observed returns between the spikes, there are two possibilities, as shown in Figure 3.2. When the stock is frequently traded, the extrapolation from the spotlight makes the observed returns more strongly covariant with the dominant macro variables than they would be if full information were available. In this case, the shadows screen out most of the firm-specific events that would otherwise reduce the portfolio's overall risk. What investors obtain in the shadows are returns which follow the macro environment more closely than the firms' intrinsic value.

On the other hand, in the presence of infrequent thin trading, which tends to be the rule rather than the exception in the shadows, there are insufficient observed returns to reflect the extrapolation from the spotlight. This does not mean that there is no extrapolation. Investors continue to form their expectations between information releases in the shadows by extrapolating from the spotlight. The lack of trading merely makes the extrapolation virtually impossible to observe in the historical data. In terms of their expectations, however, investors are exposed to systematic extrapolation risk in the shadows regardless of the stock's trading frequency.

Observation Problem

Unfortunately, the observation problem can not be resolved by shortening the estimation period and measuring returns on a daily basis. Richard Roll carried out an experiment of this kind, while looking for an explanation of the small firm effect. Although he was not dealing with neglected firms per se, he observed that the traditional market beta of small firms dropped sharply as the measurement period was shortened to a day; the impact on the beta of large firms was very much less pronounced. Roll attributed his findings to the possibility that smaller firms are thinly traded. When securities are infrequently traded, the standard estimate of beta is distorted downwards even in the absence of extrapolation risk. In effect, the lack of trading quotes reduces the measured correlation between the stocks and the market. Thus, in addition to missing the extrapolation risk, historical betas based on daily trading are biased even further downward because they do not completely capture the correlation effect.

The downward bias in historically measured betas is compounded by the intermittent return spikes that interfere with the traditional procedures for estimating systematic risk. Traditional measurement periods of 60 months, say, may encompass 20 quarterly earnings announcements with corresponding return spikes. The latter reduce the measured correlation of neglected stock returns with the market return and other macro variables. The interference of the return spikes is difficult to eliminate, since there is no way of determining how much of the spike is caused by the disclosure of historically accumulated earning changes, versus changes induced by current market conditions. The combination of thin trading and return spikes makes it virtually impossible to measure extrapolation risk.

Role of Disclosure Bias

In addition, extrapolation risk may be stronger on the downside, because it is aggravated by disclosure bias on the part of neglected firms. From the corporate treasurer's viewpoint, being in the shadows is a definite disadvantage. The shadows raise the cost of financing by the amount of the scarce information premium corresponding to the superior return on neglected firms. As discussed in the Appendix, treasurers have several ways of trying to avoid the scarce information premium. They can use retained earnings, rely on old financial friends like bankers who know the company well, or, alternatively, attract attention by releasing information in a financial marketing campaign.

In making a choice of methods, the firm has an incentive to voluntarily release information only when the news is good. In this case, management believes the market is too pessimistic and the firm is undervalued. By releasing good news about natural events, like an exciting new product line, the company may be able to get the attention of analysts, thereby moving itself from the shadows into the spotlight. Considerations of competitive advantage and other costs, however, may make information release uneconomical. In particular, when the company believes it is overvalued, it makes more sense to issue equity than to tell the market to lower its expectations.

Investors and portfolio managers, on the other hand, are aware of this game and make allowance for it. In the absence of good news, they assume that the firm may not have information worth releasing. The implication is that the firm may be suppressing negative information. Consequently, returns are biased downwards. More specifically, when the economy or industry is in bad shape, they will assume that the firm is suffering too and attempt to adjust its price accordingly. This hypothesis is consistent with recent comments on General Motors, for example. Although by no means neglected in 1986, GM apparently has not been very cooperative with analysts. According to Doron P. Levin, a staff writer with the *Wall Street Journal*, GM's relative lack of disclosure forces "analysts to be more cautious about recommending GM common shares. . . . Analysts say the difference shows up in GM's share price." As Ronald Glantz of Montgomery Securities puts it, "GM would be selling for $100 a share (rather than $71 a share) if we could believe the company's claims." Given the importance of disclosure bias even in the spotlight, it is clear that the process will play an equally critical, if not larger, role in the pricing of stocks in the shadows.

Putting it briefly, disclosure bias encourages investors to extrapolate their negative expectations into the shadows, causing greater downside systematic risk for neglected firms. In effect, disclosure bias aggravates the extrapolation risk caused by the intermittent arrival of information in the shadows.

SHADOW DANGER THREE: JUMP RISK

Traditional risk measurement assumes that returns fluctuate around a stable mean. However, this flies in the face of the dynamic reality which shows up in return series over time, both for individual stocks and at the level of the market as a whole. Discontinuous shifts in the mean of the market return distribution have been described in theoretical terms and documented empirically. Even cursory examination of market returns, using the data of Ibbotson and Sinquefield for example, suggests that the notion of a stable mean is a precarious assumption. The mean market return during the 1930s was different from that in the 1940s, or the growth decades of the 1950s and 1960s. Similarly, the distribution of market returns associated with the stagflation of the 1970s differs from the emerging growth market of the early 1980s. However, this does not mean that jumps occur once every decade. Their timing cannot be predicted; the interval between jumps may be of the order of weeks or months rather than years.

Environmental Shifts and Firm Size

How do major shifts in the macro environment affect the systematic risk perceived by investors? In the information spotlight, stock prices adjust rapidly, no matter how large the changes in the environment. The spotlight is mostly populated by companies which have highly diversified businesses and entrenched product lines. In addition, companies in the spotlight tend to have superior management which is more likely to successfully steer their company through the rough times of an environmental shock. Thus, the intrinsic value of a larger company, headed by a more experienced managerial staff, is likely to change more rapidly and relatively smoothly during periodic shocks to the system.

In the shadows, by contrast, companies are often small and

tend to have fewer and less experienced managers. Small companies, with a greater chance for mismanagement of undiversified business portfolios, are much more susceptible to the vicissitudes of environmental change than larger companies. The small computer company, for example, is much more prone to environmental buffeting than a diversified computer manufacturer. Thus, jumps in the environment may cause proportionately greater changes in small firm returns, compared to large firms. Not surprisingly, therefore, even the traditional estimates of systematic risk increase with declining firm size (see Chapter 2).

Observation Problem

Unfortunately, the impact of these jumps on systematic risk is very difficult to measure by using historical data. The combined impact of jumps and intermittent information in the shadows makes it virtually impossible to capture their effect over a definite measurement period, because the observed jumps are very infrequent and differ greatly in magnitude. For this reason, standard measurements of beta are incapable of reflecting the risk implicit in such return patterns. Insofar as the impact of the jump on observed returns is proportionately no greater than that of more continuous fluctuations, which is the case in the information spotlight, this is of little consequence. However, when the jump impact is proportionately greater, which seems to be the case for the more interesting neglected firms in the shadows, the omission of jump risk seriously understates the systematic risk to which investors are exposed.

Apart from the difficulty of capturing jump risk, historically based risk estimates do not include the other information, like that contained in analysts' earnings forecasts, which are available to investors. In Chapter 5, we shall use the variation in analysts' forecasts to obtain a measure of both the perceived jump risk and the extrapolation risk. At this point, it is sufficient to note that investors are almost certainly aware, intuitively, of the systematic instability in neglected stock returns. Therefore, it is highly unlikely that the traditional beta estimates are used to estimate risk in the shadows without an intuitive adjustment reflecting the future jump and extrapolation risk.

APPARENT DISCOUNTS

Figure 3.3 illustrates the impact of extrapolation and jump risk on the expected performance of neglected stocks in the absence of research. As in Figure 3.1, returns are on the vertical axis and systematic risk on the horizontal axis. The shadow systematic risk, β_{shadow}, is the sum of the systematic extrapolation and jump risks. The systematic risk perceived by investors before doing any research can be represented by the addition of the historical and shadow betas as shown on the horizontal axis. The inclusion of this shadow risk moves the center of the expected performance of neglected stocks from the historically observed position on to the trade-off line between risk and return. Since the estimation errors associated with expected performance may be either positive or negative, their range is depicted by the circle around the most likely risk-return position of the neglected firm on the trade-off line.

Is anything left of the shadow effect after these risks are taken into account? If the systematic risk that investors perceive before doing any research in the shadows corresponds to what one would predict from the risk-return trade-off, then the discounts on shadow stocks may be more apparent than real. Indeed, the situation in

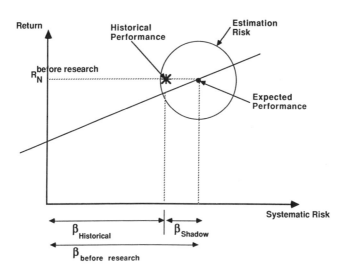

Figure 3.3   Expected performance of neglected stocks in absence of research.

Figure 3.3 can be boiled down to a restatement of the old adage: There is no such thing as a free lunch. The inclusion of extrapolation and jump risk increases the systematic risk perceived by investors to the point where it offsets the superior returns available in the shadows. Investors are aware of the special risks they face in the shadows and price neglected stocks accordingly.

In the more elaborate language of the efficient market hypothesis, Figure 3.3 suggests that capital asset prices embody all the publicly available information. Using another idiom, neglected stocks might be said to pursue a random walk down Wall Street quite similar to researched stocks. The main difference consists in large changes of direction from time to time, reflecting the cumulative response to the arrival of intermittent firm specific information and/or the sensitivity to discontinuities in the economic environment. In between these episodic return jumps, the investment community lacks the information to see clearly in the shadows. So it tends to project the returns on stocks in the spotlight onto comparable stocks in the shadows.

Real discounts can exist only relative to information which is not generally known, information that can be obtained only by research. Without engaging in security research to pierce the gloom of the shadows and find out what is actually going on, investors probably cannot expect any more from investing in the shadows than the spotlight. As discussed in Chapter 2, the historical measurement of systematic risk will reveal apparently superior returns. But investment is about future expectations that incorporate all the perceived risk in the shadows, including special dangers like extrapolation and jump risk. On average, therefore, in the absence of further security research, one might argue that neglected stocks will tend to perform according to the perceived risk-return trade-off.

If the shadow effect is more apparent than real, why all the noise about the neglected firm and other contrarian strategies? Instead of kidding oneself about superior returns, one might be better advised to follow the passive strategy of investing in a diversified market portfolio of researched and neglected stocks. But all of this assumes that shadow risk totally offsets the greater shadow returns. More importantly, it completely ignores how security research can be used to reduce risk in the shadows while exploiting the superior returns.

ROLE OF SECURITY RESEARCH

Security research is like a pocket flashlight: useless in the presence
of a bright spotlight, potentially invaluable in the dark shadows.
The purpose of security research, whether fundamental or technical, is to reduce the uncertainty surrounding the anticipated performance of stocks. When information is perfect and complete as
in the spotlight, additional research adds little if any value to what
investors already know. Conversely, the value of research is greater
in the shadows where information is scarce and uncertainty high.
In Figure 3.1, the differences in estimation risk, or uncertainty, between the spotlight and the shadows were illustrated schematically
by the circles around the expected performance of the researched
and neglected stocks. The chances of research revealing highly
abnormal performance, either above or below the risk-return line,
are vastly greater in the shadows where the estimation risk is larger.

Another way of looking at the potential benefits of research is
to say that investors have the best chances of developing a sustainable competitive advantage in those segments of the information
market that are least competitive. Although institutions may be
structurally constrained to compete against one another in the same
sectors of the information market, the simple economics of competition suggest that those with a choice are better advised to avoid
the spotlight, insofar as their operating guidelines permit.

Shadow Research Opportunities

What are the research opportunities in the shadows? Consider
the main activities in the security research industry as depicted in
Figure 3.4, together with the relative degrees of competition within
those activities in the spotlight and the shadows. In its first phase,
security research involves the collection and ferreting out of information, which is followed in the second phase, by the evaluation
and analysis of the information, and in the third phase, by pricing
and investment decision. Now compare the possibilities for developing a competitive investment advantage across these three phases
in the spotlight and the shadows.

The third phase, involving pricing decisions, does not offer

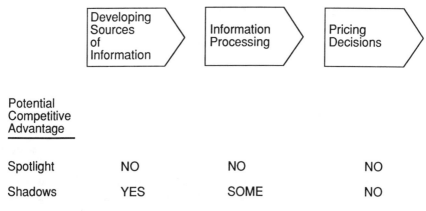

Figure 3.4   Security research process.

much opportunity for creating an advantage in either the spotlight or the shadows. Pricing decisions reflect whatever value has been associated with the information that is available. Given the processed information, investors are likely to make as many positive as negative errors in attaching a final price to it. There's not much opportunity for gaining an advantage by concentrating on the actual price-setting process itself.

With respect to information processing during the second phase of the research process, it may be possible to create an investment advantage by developing judgment-related information-processing skills, based on experience in targeted shadow sectors. Fundamental valuation models, computer software, and technical analysis are only as good as the quality of the information input. In the spotlight, where the competition is intense, enduring analytical advantages are virtually nonexistent. In the case of the dark shadows, on the other hand, it is difficult to research the kind of standardized information needed for many computer-based or quantitative investment methods. Consequently, judgment plays an important part in the processing of deep shadows information and may provide the basis for developing a competitive advantage. A good example is provided by the heavy dose of judgment that goes into the analysis of successful venture capital projects.

The best opportunities for the creation of competitive investment advantages, however, are provided by the first phase of the research process, involving the search for information. In the shadows the low levels of institutional and analyst activity leave the field open to investors, portfolio managers, and entrepeneurial analysts willing to put the effort into the generation of useful information sources. The 80/20 rule associated with declining returns to information can be fully exploited in the shadows, insofar as the first 20 percent of the information, yielding 80 percent of the benefit from security research, is rarely in place. Shadow researchers have the best chance of laying their hands on that first critical 20 percent of information that is needed to identify a real discount.

Taking the research process as a whole, fundamental and technical methods really make sense only in the shadows. In the spotlight, the name of the game is to keep up with the investment competition. Fundamental and/or technical research can provide only transient advantages, because the intensity of the competition quickly reduces the returns on research. By contrast, in the shadows, fundamental research based on new information sources can play a crucial role in reducing the uncertainty surrounding neglected securities, while technical research may assist in anticipating the timing of shifts between the spotlight and the shadows.

REAL DISCOUNTS

Security research pays off when it uncovers stocks that are not on the risk-return trade-off line. For example, research may show that the stock's risk is greater or less than implicit in the market trade-off. Alternatively, the firm's true performance may suggest a return above or below the market line.

Beware of Lemons

Overall, two kinds of practical situations are possible. First, the information may indicate that the stock is overvalued. When this information is added to what was previously available, instead of an expected performance consistent with the market's risk-return relationship, the stock falls below the line with substandard performance, as shown in Figure 3.5. In this case, research yields a lower return and/or higher risk estimate than anticipated prior to the research effort. By analogy with the duds found in other markets, these shadow securities can be called lemons.

When a lemon is correctly identified, its true risk-return performance is inferior. If not picked up by other players, perhaps because the true risk is difficult to measure, the security will continue to exhibit inferior behavior. Continuing performance below par means that returns are insufficient to cover the true risk, which is symptomatic of possible impending bankruptcy. Unfortunately, share prices only react slowly to possible business failure. Although the available studies have not discriminated between the spotlight and the shadows, the chances are that the price adjustment process is particularly sluggish for poorly performing, neglected firms. Investors and managers, therefore, will want to avoid an unrecognized, overpriced lemon.

On the other hand, if a lemon is widely recognized as such, its price will drop, providing an opportunity for short trading, until the return and risk are again consistent with the market standard. Yet, short trading opportunities seem to be the exception rather than the rule, especially in the shadows. Owing to thin trading and the

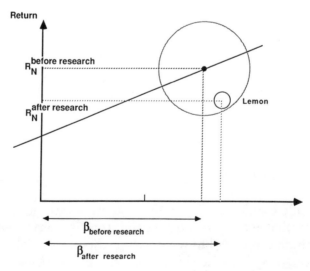

Figure 3.5   Security research: Uncovering a lemon.

relatively small capitalization of stocks in the shadows, profitable short trading will rarely occur.

Discovering a Discount Stock

The second possibility is that research may turn up information suggesting that the stock is underpriced. In this case, the expected performance is above the line, with higher return and/or lower risk than anticipated prior to the research effort, as shown in Figure 3.6. These can be called discount stocks, where the discount is not apparent but real, and the stock is worth more than its market price.

The correct indentification of a discount stock is the much sought-after prize in security research. The investor, or manager, uses security research and comes up with a forecast which differs positively from the consensus embodied in the current share price. The price of the stock may not move much, if the discount is not widely recognized and the consensus valuation does not change. Nevertheless, the investment manager may earn above average risk-adjusted returns, if the perceived risk after research is less than that implied by the market line.

Of course, the big payoff occurs when the discount becomes

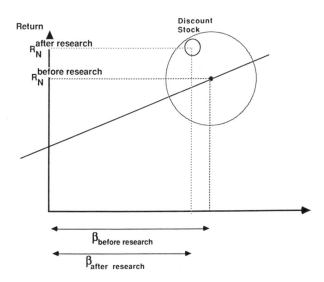

Figure 3.6   Security research: Uncovering a discount stock.

more widely recognized and the consensus forecast shifts. Depending on how rapidly the consensus changes, the price rise may be gradual, or come in a jump. Either way the original investor reaps the large, one-time return associated with a reequilibration of the stock's price incorporating the more positive expectations. The process of expectations realignment has been examined by several authors, for example, by Elton, Gruber, and Gultekin, who conclude: "Larger excess returns are earned if one is able to determine those stocks for which analysts most underestimate return. The largest returns can be earned by knowing the stocks for which analysts will make the greatest revision in their estimates. Given any degree of forecasting ability, managers can obtain the best results by acting on the difference between their forecasts and the consensus forecast."

What these authors do not explore is where investors have the best chance of developing a superior "forecasting ability." The central argument of Part I of this book is that investors have by far the best opportunities for so doing in the shadows, rather than the spotlight. Indeed, one can say there are essentially only two broad investment strategies: One may invest in the spotlight by buying a piece of the market portfolio as academics would advise. With this choice, one makes no attempt to beat the market averages. Security research, while needed for portfolio maintenance, is of dubious competitive advantage in the glare of the information spotlight. The second option is to invest in the shadows. Here investors can take an active approach to investing, ferreting out discount stocks with security research. The darker the shadow, the greater the chance of developing a competitive investment advantage.

The evidence and the theory clearly show that, of the two broad investment arenas, the shadows are by far more suited to an active approach. The pressing question, addressed in Part II, is how to proceed with research in the shadows, to exploit the possibilities available in that sector of the market for outperforming the market averages.

PART II

PIERCING THE SHADOWS

This section describes how security research can be applied in the shadows. The emphasis is on the unique aspects of shadow research. Chapter 4 describes the first step, the identification of neglected stocks. Once identified, the stock's reward-to-risk ratio must be researched to see whether it is a true discount stock. Chapter 5 discusses risk assessment in the shadows, together with the estimation of a new beta. Shadow approaches to fundamental research are developed in Chapter 6, while Chapter 7 concentrates on statistical analysis. Taken together, Chapters 5, 6, and 7 provide the methods needed to decide whether a neglected stock is indeed a true discount stock. If so, Chapter 8 describes how analysts' attention can be monitored to assess whether a discount stock will be recognized and emerge from the shadows into the spotlight.

4

IDENTIFYING NEGLECTED STOCKS

Identifying neglected stocks is the necessary first step in the process of exploiting the superior returns available in the shadows of Wall Street. This chapter contrasts five different approaches that can be employed to search for neglected stocks. To a large extent, these approaches are derived from the empirical research described in Chapter 2. They are presented in order of increasing closeness to the activity of security analysts, because the latter bears the closest relationship to future shadow returns.

NUMBER OF SHAREHOLDERS

What is it that classifies a company's stock as neglected? Are the shadows best described in a black and white context, or is it more realistic to consider information availability as an attribute which varies in a more continuous fashion across securities? A company is classified as neglected if it has very little information available on it in the market. However, one can be certain that no stock exists about which nothing is known. If this is true, then neglect can be defined only in a relative manner in terms of how little is known about a stock.

If one were asked to identify the company with the least public information, it most assuredly would be a newly formed private sole proprietorship. In this setting there is only one "super insider" who possesses all the information about the company. Barring any leaks by the IRS and the like, whatever information that individual chooses to release would be the only information available to outsiders. Such firms, the ultimate in neglect, are shrouded in the darkest shadows. Nevertheless, they form a major hunting ground for venture capitalists, who are the most extreme of shadow investors.

Taking a step towards the spotlight, one finds partnerships, where several partners each have the insider's track on information about the company. Next comes corporations, where there are proportionately as many owners or shareholders as there are shares outstanding. The intensity of the spotlight increases dramatically as one moves to the publicly traded corporation. The theme that ties these examples together is the increasing number of shareholders at each level of ownership. The difference between the level of information available to insiders, compared to that of the outsiders, declines as we move from the shadows into the spotlight. However, even among publicly traded corporations, which are of primary interest to us here, there is a great disparity in the number of insiders.

The Securities and Exchange Commission defines insiders as corporate directors and individuals who own more than 5 percent of the outstanding shares of a company's stock. To be considered an insider of IBM, an individual would have to own in excess of 30 million shares of IBM. However, to be an insider of International Royalty of Oil (IROC on the over-the-counter market (OTC)) an investor would need to own a little more than 120,000 shares. By the SEC definition, there are likely to be proportionately more insiders in IROC than in IBM.

Looking at the situation from the other side of the coin, we see that IBM is likely to have many more shareholders than IROC. Each shareholder who receives annual reports and other information on the company represents a point of potential information dissemination. Hence, more information is available in the market on companies with greater numbers of shareholders. The greater the number of shareholders, the less neglected a company is likely to be. The hypothetical extreme is where all investors in the market own shares in the company's stock.

According to the 1985 NYSE Fact Book, as of mid-1983, fully 25 percent of all adult Americans own stock. This translates into more than 42 million shareholders in the U.S. alone. Shareownership rose sharply between mid-1981 and mid-1983 with 10.1 million people adding stocks to their holdings of assets. The stock which had the largest number of shareholders of record on December 31, 1984 was post-breakup AT&T, with about 3.2 million shareholders. AT&T, the most widely held company, is owned by about 8 percent of all possible shareholders. IBM, with about 800,000 shareholders, is held by only 2 percent of all shareholders.

Exactly when a stock becomes relatively neglected according to this criterion depends on how active the shareholders are. As a rough guide, it would not be unreasonable to say that any company with less than 8000 shareholders, one percent of IBM's number, could be considered neglected. In other words, when less than 0.02 percent of all shareholders own stock in a company, it might be considered a neglected stock corresponding to research concentration ranking 3 in Chapter 2.

Information on shareholders becomes known only once a year, and as such it is not a very sensitive measure of neglect. If there is a large increase in shares, or a drop in the total number of share-holders during the year, one must wait until the year-end data becomes available to determine the actual shift in relative neglect for a particular stock. As a cross check, this criterion for neglect is useful but, because of its roughness and time-insensitivity, should not be used as a primary indicator of neglect.

The best source for shareholder information is the COMPU-STAT II computerized investment service. COMPUSTAT II contained information on over 6000 publicly traded companies in 1986, including all NYSE, most ASE, and over 3500 over-the-counter stocks. Fully half of the companies included in the service have annual sales under $100 million, ensuring a wide selection of neglected companies. Although the computer service is updated on a weekly basis, the information on the number of common shareholders is available only annually. Since companies have different fiscal year-ends, the updated data for all companies contains some revisions each week.

RELATIVE VOLUME AND LARGE BLOCK TRADING

Every time a trade takes place in the market, information is transmitted regarding the perceived value of the stock in question. Prices will always adjust to reflect the market's consensus in response to the latest trade. Brokers, floor traders, and market makers are all a part of this process. They, in turn, will incorporate the information disseminated as a result of the trade into their valuation of the stock and will transmit that information along their information networks to all interested parties.

Therefore, stocks which are actively traded will have more information available on a more current and continuous basis than stocks which are thinly traded. Several studies have shown that the mere assessment of a stock's systematic market risk is a problematic task for thinly traded stocks (see Chapter 3). The lack of trading makes it difficult to assess the true correlation between a stock and the market. Trading activity is thus closely related to both the level and interpretation of information available on a stock.

Similarly, large block trading, the disposition of 10,000 share lots, translates into more information than the trading of small or odd lots. Large block trading echoes institutional trading in the market. If a stock is held and traded regularly by large institutional investors, then it will have numerous large block transactions on any given day. As these large blocks are traded, information is disseminated in the marketplace regarding the etiology of the trade. Trading for liquidity purposes will carry little information, while trades for valuation reasons carry potent information.

A stock's relative trading frequency and volume, as well as the number of large block transactions per day, are indicators of relative neglect in the stock market. Relative rather than absolute volume is the key, because over the last 30 years, volume on the stock exchanges has increased more than thirty-fold. From 1952 to 1980, public volume, excluding stock exchange member trading, has increased from 2.6 million to 71.4 million shares per day. Institutional trading over that same period has increased from 800,000 shares per day in 1952 to over 46 million shares per day in 1980. This increase has moved institutional trading from 30.8 percent to almost 65 percent of the trading volume per day on the NYSE.

Since most institutions trade with large block transactions, the frequency of NYSE large block transactions has grown simultaneously. The growth of these institutional footprints has increased dramatically over the last 20 years. During 1965, there were only 2171 large block transactions, or about 9 per day. This represented only 3.1 percent of all trading in the market. During 1984, however, there were 433,427 large block transactions, or about 1713 per day. This represented about 50 percent of the volume on the NYSE that year. In fact, there were almost as many large block transactions in one day in 1984 (1713) as there were during all of 1965 (2171).

Since both share volume and large block trading have increased over the years, it is important to think in terms of relatives. A stock that was classified as frequently traded in 1960 would have exhibited much less trading activity than a stock that is classified as frequently traded today. Moreover, a stock with a 100 million share float would most likely trade more frequently, with more large block transactions, than would a stock with a 1 million float.

The most appropriate measures of neglect in this context are relative volume and relative large block trading. The stock's daily trading volume as a percent of its float relative to the same ratio for the market as a whole, or relative to a bench mark, like the daily trading of IBM, can be used as a measure of this information proxy. Once again it is a judgment call, but a stock whose trading represents less than one percent of the relative daily volume of IBM, say, would be a good candidate for a neglected stock in the sense of Chapter 2.

The two best sources for this information, on a timely basis, are Standard & Poor's Marketscope, which is available on the Quotron system, and Media General Financial Services Database, which is available through the Dow Jones News/Retrieval service. Marketscope provided information on over 4600 companies in 1986, including the average daily volume for each stock. Media General, which provided access to data on over 4300 companies, also included data on trading volume.

In addition, Media General, through the Dow Jones system, allows for easy comparison of these volume statistics within industry groups and across different companies. This makes the determination of relative neglect much easier. By taking the average daily volume as a percentage of the outstanding shares (also available on the system) and dividing that figure by the same value for IBM, one obtains the stock's relative trading volume as a percentage of its outstanding shares. Since these data bases are updated on a daily basis, they provide a dynamic assessment of a stock's relative neglect in the market.

PERIOD OF LISTING

The period of time which has elapsed since a stock has been listed on the exchange is also a proxy for the amount of information available in the market. Companies that have been listed for a long time are mature and have an established information network through which to transmit important news. On the other hand, firms that have been listed for only a short period of time have not built up this kind of network, and hence have less information disseminated about them on a regular basis.

The period of listing effect, discussed in Chapter 2, dealt only with stocks on the NYSE. Moreover, stocks listed for only a short time on the exchange were omitted from the study, due to the problems associated with shifting from other exchanges. The results of that study do not imply that stocks listed for the same period on the ASE, say, and the NYSE have the same level of information available. They imply only that, for stocks on the NYSE, the shorter listing periods indicated less available information. The period of listing should be used, therefore, relative to the market in question. If one wishes to compare stocks within the same exchange for their degree of neglect, the period of listing within the exchange provides a proxy for information availability. However, this proxy should not be employed to determine the relative neglect of stocks on the NYSE, compared to those listed on the ASE, or the OTC/NASDAQ markets.

Information on a stock's period of listing is available through each stock exchange's office or through the SEC. It is not readily available on any widely used computerized investment services to our knowledge, but may be available through Disclosure for some companies. Owing to its relative inaccessibility, the listing period should be used only as a check, when there are some discrepancies among the other measures of neglect discussed in this chapter.

INSTITUTIONAL HOLDINGS

Not only has institutional trading become an increasingly important factor in the pricing process of the NYSE, but with their increased trading activity, institutions are now among the most sophisticated investors in the stock market. Driven by legal, managerial, and structural requirements, institutions are also among the most risk-averse investors. Until about fifteen years ago, most of their investments were concentrated among the "blue chips." However, a dramatic increase in the funds under management has forced institutions to move beyond this limited subset of securities.

Table 4.1 reports on the estimated holdings of some selected institutional investors. In 1955 institutions held about $31 billion worth of stocks in the NYSE. This represented 15 percent of the total market value of the NYSE. In 1980, this figure exploded to $440.2 billion worth of stock, representing well over 35 percent of the total market value of all stocks listed on the NYSE. This growth was fueled by the tremendous increase in pension fund assets, which grew from $3.5 billion to almost $220 billion.

The fact that institutions needed to increase the scope of their holdings due to the growth of funds under management has not

TABLE 4.1 Institutional Holdings of NYSE Stock ($ Billions)

Type of Institution	1955	1960	1965	1970	1975	1980
U.S. institutions:						
Insurance companies:						
Life	$ 2.2	$ 3.2	$ 6.3	$ 11.7	$ 21.6	$ 38.1
Nonlife	4.2	6.0	10.1	12.2	11.6	26.9
Investment companies:						
Open-end	6.3	12.4	29.1	39.0	35.0	38.1
Close-end	4.6	4.2	5.6	4.1	5.5	5.1
Noninsured pension funds:						
Corporate & other private	3.4	14.3	35.9	60.7	82.5	166.0
State & local government	0.1	0.3	1.4	9.6	24.4	53.0
Nonprofit institutions:						
Foundations	6.9	8.0	16.4	17.0	20.8	32.4
Educational endowments	2.3	2.9	5.9	6.6	7.7	12.1
Common trust funds	0.9	1.4	3.2	4.1	5.2	9.5
Mutual savings banks	0.2	0.2	0.5	1.4	2.4	1.5
Subtotal	$ 31.1	$ 52.9	$114.4	$166.4	$216.7	$ 382.7
Foreign institutions	N/A	N/A	N/A	N/A	25.1	57.5
Total	$ 31.1	$ 52.9	$114.4	$636.4	$241.8	$ 440.2
Market value of all NYSE-listed stock	$207.7	$307.0	$537.5	$636.4	$685.1	$1,242.8
Estimated % held by institutional investors	15%	17.2%	21.3%	26.1%	35.3%	35.4%

N/A: not available
Source: *NYSE Factbook* (1985). Reprinted with permission.

meant that these investors have become careless. On the contrary, institutional investors, after moving away from the top 50 companies, have expended increasing amounts of time and money researching their investments. As institutional investors moved into more stocks, they carried with them teams of research analysts to analyze these investments. The level of information available on these stocks increased correspondingly.

The stock with the largest institutional interest in the market, again, is IBM. More than 1600 institutions own more than 300 million shares of IBM. This represents almost 50 percent of IBM's outstanding shares. By contrast, International Royalty and Oil was owned by no institutions as of December 1984. There are thousands of stocks in the market, at any instant, which are owned by very few or no institutions. These are the institutionally neglected stocks, which are of primary interest to investors in the shadows.

The Securities and Exchange Commission requires all institutional investors (banks, insurance companies, college endowments, pension funds, and the like) managing over $100 million to submit a 13F report of all equity holdings within 45 days of the close of each quarter of operation. As a result of these filings, both the number of institutions holding shares in a particular stock and the total number of shares held by these institutions are available on a fairly timely basis.

How many institutions need to own stock before it begins to move out of the shadows? How many shares need they own? As a rule of thumb, a stock that is owned by fewer than five institutions can normally be classified as neglected in the sense of Chapter 2. This criterion should be supplemented, however, by the percentage of outstanding shares owned by the institutions. Ownership of less than five percent of the outstanding shares by institutions can be considered necessary to classify a stock as neglected. Proportionately, this represents institutional ownership equal to one-tenth of the institutional ownership of IBM. If these two criteria agree, the stock is neglected. If not, further research is necessary.

One example of conflicting signals from these criteria is in the case of Land of Lincoln Savings and Loan (LOLS OTC) and Land Resources (LRES OTC) in early 1986. Both these stocks had the same number of institutions holding stock (two) and about the same number of shares outstanding (approximately three million). However, LOLS had 10 percent institutional share ownership and LRES less than 3 percent. According to the criteria cited above, Land of Lincoln Savings and Loan would not necessarily be considered institutionally neglected, whereas Land Resources would be. To obtain a more conclusive rating of LOLS's level of neglect in the market, further research, based on the other measures of neglect discussed in this chapter, would be needed.

In general, however, the number of institutions holding a stock and the percentage of all outstanding shares held by institutions are likely to be highly correlated. It is reasonable to assume that the greater the number of institutional holdings, the more shares held by institutions. Moreover, since each institution holding a stock is a source of information transmission in the market, there will be more monitoring of those securities on a timely basis. Therefore, both the number of institutions holding shares and the percentage of the outstanding shares held by institutions are appropriate measures of available information.

On the other hand, institutions are required to report their holdings only quarterly, and have a 45-day grace period. Thus, a change in institutional holding can take as long as 135 days (90 days plus the 45-day grace period) to filter through the system. Moreover, if an institution moves in and out of a stock within a quarter, it is not reflected in the 13F report. Although this may reduce the level of confidence in institutional holdings as an indicator of market neglect somewhat, it does not diminish its importance as a reflection of the general intensity of the investment spotlight on any given stock.

Institutional holdings and the percentage of shares held by institutions are available through a number of sources. Disclosure, a reporting system which gathers the output of most SEC filings, has the data available on its Disclosure II computerized data base. The other main source of this data is Vickers, a division of ARGUS Research. Since the analysis of institutional interest is one of the primary functions of the Vickers service, their data is both more comprehensive and user-friendly than Disclosure II. However, Disclosure II had a wider base of information with more than 8900 companies included in the service in 1986, compared to about 7500 common stocks covered by the Vickers service. In addition to these sources, Standard and Poor's reports the information in their monthly stock guide, as well as in their computerized investment analysis package, STOCKPAK II. Compustat also has the information available on their computerized service COMPUSTAT II.

ANALYST ATTENTION

The level of analysts' attention is by far the most direct measure of information availability in the market. Analysts are directly responsible for ferreting out and interpreting data, as well as disseminating its meaning in the form of forecasts. Analysts provide the link between firms and the information available concerning them. The more analysts there are who provide opinions on a company's performance, the more information is disseminated in the market. Among all the proxies discussed in this chapter, a company's level of analyst attention will, more than any other factor, ultimately determine the level of available information.

As of June 1986, there were well over 2500 security analysts in the North America working for more than 130 brokerage firms and research institutions. These analysts provide information on over 3400 companies listed on the NYSE, the ASE, and the OTC. In addition, numerous estimates are provided on companies listed on the Toronto and London Stock Exchange, providing information to investors desiring to expand their portfolio holdings into international markets. These analysts provide earnings-per-share estimates for one and two years into the future and five-year earnings growth estimates. The forecasts are used by analysts, investors, and managers, in turn, to determine the relative under- or overvaluation of stocks in the market. Stocks that are ignored by the analysts prove to be more difficult to identify as under- or overvalued.

Even among those stocks that are followed by security analysts there is a great deal of variability in the quantity of information available. As discussed in Chapter 1, analysts' attention is not evenly distributed among all securities covered. Moreover, in some cases there may be the same number of analysts providing forecasts for the next year's earnings per share and a very different number providing forecasts for two years ahead. For example, in January 1986, Burnham Service Corp. (BSCO, OTC) had six analysts providing forecasts for December 1986 and only one analyst providing a forecast for December 1987. In contrast, Parker Pen Corp. (PKR, NYSE) had six forecasts for both 1986 and 1987.

In addition, five-year growth forecasts are not always provided for companies, even with a high level of analyst coverage one and two years out. Take the case of Bowater Inc. (BOW, NYSE), which in 1986 had eleven analysts providing forecasts for each of the next two years. Bowater, for some reason, did not have a projected five-year growth rate provided by analysts. On the other hand, Brush-Wellman (BW, NYSE), with eleven forecasts for each of the next two year's earnings, did have a five-year earnings growth rate reported.

The result is a wide spectrum of information availability. The shadows cannot be described as purely black and white. There is a considerable amount of gray in between the darkest informational shadows and the brightest spotlight. Using analysts' attention, one could define the shadows as those companies having no forecasts at all. Since there were forecasts for only 3400 companies in 1986, the shadows of Wall Street were crowded with neglected stocks.

If the shadows are defined as including only stocks with zero analysts' coverage, what of all the stocks with one or two analysts covering them? How about those companies with one analyst providing a forecast for next year, but no forecast for two years out and no five-year forecast? Clearly the shadows include not only the thousands of securities with no estimates provided by analysts, but some stocks with one, two, or maybe three analysts covering them. It all depends on how strictly the investor wishes to define the concept of neglect.

The number of analysts necessary to classify a stock as researched was discussed at length in Chapter 2. It was shown that the tighter the definition of neglect, the stronger the neglected firm effect, and the greater the returns that can be anticipated from shadow investment. Using the most comprehensive data, having more than nine analysts in Chapter 2 classified a stock as highly researched, while having less than three classified it as neglected. Stocks in between were moderately researched on the fringes of the shadows.

However, like the other variables described in this chapter, measures of analysts' neglect are only proxy indicators of the informational shadow surrounding a stock. The analyst forecast services usually give equal weight to the forecasts of some of the smaller regional analysts. It is not clear what the importance of these estimates is compared to those of the larger investment houses, which wield much more power in the market. Even among the analysts of the larger investment houses, there are those whose advice carries more weight and contains more information.

The premier provider of information on analysts' estimates is I/B/E/S, the Institutional Brokers Estimate System. I/B/E/S includes estimates from almost all the active U.S. analysts and provides numerous services that integrate analysts' forecasts into a comprehensive investment service well suited for the identification of neglected stocks, both in the deep shadows and on the periphery. I/B/E/S is updated daily to provide weekly and monthly publications to subscribers. In addition, I/B/E/S offers an on-line system which provides continuously updated electronic information on analysts' forecasts.

A service very similar to I/B/E/S is produced by Zach's Investment Research and is known as The ICARUS Service. Icarus

TABLE 4.2   Proxies for Measurement of Neglect

Proxy	Reliability Rank	Approximate Neglect Cutoff	Period of Update	Source
Period of listing	5	Lowest 10% within market	Annually	SEC or Exchanges
Number of shareholders	4	1% of IBM shareholders	Annually	Compustat II
Relative volume & large block trading	3	Relative trading volume 1% of relative trading volume of IBM	Daily	S&P market scope on Quotron
Institutional holdings	2	Not more than 5 institutions and 5% of outstanding shares owned by institutions	Quarterly	Vickers, Disclosure II Stock II CDA Investment Technologies
Analyst coverage	1	Not more than 3 analysts providing forecasts for the next fiscal year	Monthly	I/B/E/S, Icarus, Drexel Burnham Lambert, S&P Earnings Forecaster

provided estimates on almost 2000 companies in 1986 obtained from over one thousand estimates. ICARUS is also available on the Dow Jones News/Retrieval service. With such cost-efficient access and the ability to cross-check other measures of neglect within the Dow Jones Service, many investors may find the Icarus service to be an excellent complement and an acceptable alternative to the I/B/E/S/ system. Other firms which provide similar, albeit less inclusive, information are Drexel Burnham Lambert's service, which included their estimates on over 1750 companies in 1986, and Standard & Poor's Earnings Forecaster, which canvassed about fifty major analysts who provided forecasts on about 1600 companies.

Although all the proxies discussed in this chapter are highly correlated, the true level of information availability is not easily measured by one variable. For this reason, no single measure or proxy should be used in isolation to identify neglected stocks. Instead, portfolio managers and investors are strongly advised to check all indicators to determine the most likely level of available information. Table 4.2 summarizes the proxies discussed in this chapter. Each proxy is ranked in order of importance in terms of its reliability as an indicator of neglect (5 = lowest, 1 = highest). Next the level that approximately corresponds to the third category of neglect in Chapter 2 is listed along with the periodicity, or frequency of update, and the sources that can be used to locate and analyze each proxy.

5

ASSESSING RISK IN THE SHADOWS

Scarce information in the shadows makes it difficult to assess the true risk in a stock's return. Whereas Chapter 3 provided the theoretical underpinnings of shadow risk, the issue in this chapter is how to assess the magnitude of, and begin to deal with that risk. First both qualitative and quantitative approaches to assessing environmentally induced systematic risk are discussed. In particular, a new beta incorporating analysts' forecasts is introduced to capture some of the systematic shadow risk. Second, the limited potential for diversification as a way of reducing company-specific risk in the shadows leads to consideration of bankruptcy ratios and company analysis as ways of assessing that risk.

ENVIRONMENTAL INSTABILITY

To what extent can a portfolio be protected from systematic shadow risk? Systematic risk is a reflection of environmental fluctuations that cannot be diversified away by forming a portfolio. The investor's exposure to systematic risk in the shadows depends, therefore, on two key questions: First, what are the potential sources and magnitude of external fluctuations? Second, what is their likely impact on stocks in the shadows?

Fluctuations in the Environment

In qualitative terms, external instability may be either random, or tied to economic cycles. Random shocks, like the oil price crisis or natural disasters, are virtually impossible to predict. Since their impact depends on the particular nature of the crisis and the type of neglected firm, there is little that can be done to protect shadow investments from them.

Economic cycles may appear to be more regular, but their critical turning points are no easier to predict. Some observers have tried to decompose the historical data into combinations of regular cycles: for example, the so-called long wave Kondratieff cycle of 50 to 60 years, plus Juglar cycles of 9 to 10 years, and Kitchin cycles of 40 months' duration. But detailed statistical analysis by the U.S. National Bureau of Economic Research finds little, if any, evidence of these. Rather, the data suggests that most of the long-run time series are affected by random fluctuations in prices that often peak during times of major war.

Apart from war, economic cycles have been attributed to innumerable causes, ranging from sunspots to psychology. Mainstream economists point to three overall explanations. First, there are forecasting errors committed by businessmen who over- or underinvest relative to the long-run real growth needs of the economy. Second, consumers shift their demands and tastes, thereby sending periodic ripple effects through the economy. Third, changes in monetary and fiscal policy on the part of government often induce variation in business and consumer behavior. Predicting the forecasting errors of the business community, the shifting tastes of consumers, or the policy of government is at best an extremely hazardous exercise, and is unlikely to contribute to risk assessment in the shadows. To the extent, therefore, that economic cycles cannot be predicted, they have to be endured.

Qualitative Assessment of Systematic Risk

However, one can try to estimate the exposure of a neglected firm to external fluctuations. This is of particular importance in the shadows, because it affects the market pricing of the firm's stock in a discontinuous fashion. Smaller neglected companies tend to exhibit exaggerated jump-type responses to changes in their environment. In addition, investors tend to extrapolate the macro fluctuations into the shadows more than into the spotlight (see Chapter 3). This risk exposure is a function of three links in the mechanism that transmits macro cycles through to a firm's earnings. Understanding these three links provides a qualitative way of assessing systematic risk in the shadows.

First, there is the cyclicality of the firm's industry, which transmits the macro fluctuations through to the industry's demand pattern. Cyclicality may be most easily assessed by using information on the industry available in the spotlight. In general, industries that depend on large or discretionary consumer outlays are more cyclical, such as the construction industry and tourism. However, the degree of cyclicality is not invariable; it depends on the nature of the macro fluctuations. A change in GNP growth rate, for example, affects mainly the demand in both high-tech and heavy industries. By contrast, interest rates have their greatest impact on the cost of funds for high-tech industry, whereas they often affect both demand and the cost of funds in heavy industry.

The competitive structure of the industry provides the second link in the transmission of macro fluctuations through to the earnings. It mediates between the change in industry demand and the variation in company sales. For the dominant company in an industry, clearly, sales fluctuations will be more or less the same as industry demand movements. But in the shadows, many of the firms are smaller players, often following unnoticed niche strategies. Here changes in overall industry demand may not be as critical. Aggressive smaller competitors may be able to offset a decline in industry demand by increasing market share. The latter is often easier to achieve in growing product market, however, when everybody is benefiting from higher demand. Alternatively, smaller players may be protected by the special factors driving niche demand. In assessing these factors, there is no substitute for detailed knowledge of the industry (see Chapter 6).

The third link in the chain consists in the operating and financial structure of the firm, which transmits sales changes into earnings variability. The leverage ratios are the key to this process. High operating leverage, due to high fixed costs, magnifies the impact of sales fluctuations, as does high financial leverage, caused by high levels of borrowing. Thus, firms in capital-intensive industries, such as chemicals and computers, especially those with heavy borrowing, tend to have higher exposure to macro cycles. Analysis of leverage provides a qualitative key to the assessment of environmentally induced systematic risk.

MEASURING SYSTEMATIC RISK

The qualitative recognition of systematic risk begs the question of the extent to which it can be quantified in the shadows. The standard beta (used in Chapter 2) to capture systematic risk is measured by estimating the volatility in the stock's return relative to that of the market index. The latter is used to reflect fluctuations in the macro environment. One of the advantages of the beta coefficient is its wide availability from several financial service firms, both in the United States and the United Kingdom. Value Line, Merrill Lynch, Media General, and others are examples of firms that produce publications containing beta estimates.

In practice, the beta coefficient has been demonstrated to vary with the cyclicality of the firm's industry and its operating and financial structure in accordance with the qualitative assessment above. A beta of one corresponds to a return volatility equal, on average, to that of the market index. Companies in highly cyclical industries, like the emerging personal computer market of 1980, have betas well above one, while those in counter cyclical industries, like alcoholic beverages in some countries, have a beta of less than one. Diversified companies, or those with markets tied into a broad cross section of the economy, such as IBM, have betas very close to unity. Similarly, diversified portfolios should also have betas close to one.

How does beta vary in the shadows? In Table 5.1 historical portfolio betas are listed by firm size for stocks in the shadows and the spotlight. It is clear that beta tends to be larger for smaller companies, owing to the lower degree of diversification in their business. Since their sales are more cyclically dependent, any shift in underlying macro factors tends to cause a pronounced shift in small cap company returns. While the historical beta increases with smaller size, it does not increase as one moves from the spotlight into the shadows. Moving down any column from closely followed to neglected companies, while keeping size constant, we see that beta declines. Apparently, scarce information in the shadows is not reflected in higher systematic risk when beta is estimated by using standard measurement techniques.

One disadvantage of applying the historical beta coefficient in the shadows is that it averages out the impact of different macro disturbances; it does not discriminate between the various factors which might be responsible for fluctuations in the market index. As

TABLE 5.1   Beta Coefficients by Size and Neglect

| Research Concentration | Size | | |
Ranking 1976–1981	Small	Medium	Large
RCR 1 Closely followed	1.483	1.264	1.026
RCR 2 Moderately followed	1.351	1.180	1.037
RCR 3 Neglected	1.282	1.089	0.934

Source: Steven Carvell, "The Impact of Analyst Neglect on Stock Market Performance," Ph.D. Dissertation, State University of New York, 1984.

suggested earlier, the shadows magnify the impact of various macro disturbances. Therefore, historical estimates of systematic risk cannot capture the true shadow risk faced by investors. The historical betas either are measured over too short a period to include the jumps and extrapolations, or are distorted by the firm's evolution when measured over too long a period. It is not surprising, then, that the statistical uncertainty associated with beta estimation increases as one moves into the shadows.

NEW BETA INCORPORATING SHADOW RISK

The reliability of the historical beta never enters into standard risk assessment procedures. Quite amazingly, no distinction is made between a beta measured with a high level of statistical confidence and one with a low level. The lack of statistical confidence in the shadows to a great extent mirrors historical jumps and past extrapolations. As a result, measures of confidence can be employed to capture part of the historical shadow risk. One of these measures is known as the standard error in the mean return. The latter will be employed as a first representation of shadow risk.

In addition, the variance in the forecasts of analysts contains information about shadow risk. Security analysts generate point estimates of future earnings and hence indirectly the expected return in the next period. The difference between the forecasts of individual analysts reflects uncertainty concerning the evolutionary nature of the company in the near future. For this reason, differences of opinion between analysts tend to increase as one moves into the shadows. The variance in analysts' forecasts, which reflects these differences in opinion, will be used below as a second way of incorporating shadow risk into the standard beta estimate.

An approximate estimate of shadow risk can be obtained by combining the standard error in the mean with the variance in analysts' forecasts. Together with the historical correlation coefficient, this shadow risk estimate can then be used to generate a new beta that reflects the lack of information in the shadows. The derivation of the new beta incorporating shadow risk is outlined in the appendix to this chapter, within the framework of the market model.

To see whether the new beta discriminates between the sys-

TABLE 5.2   New Beta Incorporating Shadow Risk

Total risk	=	Historical risk	+	Shadow risk
New* beta	=	$\left[\left(\dfrac{\text{Historical}}{\text{beta}}\right)^2\right.$	+	$\left.\left(\dfrac{\text{Shadow}}{\text{beta}}\right)^2\right]^{1/2}$

*For derivation, see Appendix to Chapter 5.

tematic risk of stocks in the spotlight and the shadows, the authors tested a random sample of 660 stocks from the NYSE. Three portfolios were constructed, each consisting of securities within a specific range of analysts' attention. Portfolio 1 consisted of the most highly researched securities, with more than 19 analysts following each stock; these also tended to be the largest companies in the sample. Portfolio 2 consisted of moderately researched securities, with between six and 19 analysts providing forecasts. Finally, Portfolio 3 was comprised of the most neglected securities in the sample; these securities tended to have the lowest market value of the securities under study. Securities with fewer than three analysts were not studied, because of the absence of sufficient forecasts necessary to compute a valid coefficient of variation. Hence, the analysis and the resulting new beta did not include stocks in the deep shadows. The results of the test are shown in Table 5.3, which compares the relative risk of the three portfolios.

    Column three reports the mean historical beta for each portfolio. Upon inspection, we observe that the traditional beta rises slightly, going from 1.038 in portfolio RCR 1 to 1.209 in RCR 3. This occurs primarily because beta tends to rise with declining market capitalization, and RCR 3 contains relatively more small-market-value securities than RCR 1.

    Column two shows that the dispersion in analysts' forecasts increases with declining analysts' attention. In fact, the coefficient of variation in RCR 3 is more than twice as large as the value in RCR 1. The effect of this on the new beta is evident in column four. We can see that the new beta rises from 1.278 in the spotlight (RCR 1) to 1.822 on the periphery on the shadows (RCR 3), an increase of almost 43 percent, whereas the traditional beta goes up by only 16 percent. The greater rise in the new beta is due entirely to the shadow risk embodied in the neglected portfolio. Thus, on passing

TABLE 5.3 Shadow Risk Impact on Beta

Research Concentration Ranking 1976–1981	Average Number of Analysts	Coefficient of Variation	Historical Beta	New Beta
RCR 1 Closely followed	22	.05	1.038	1.278
RCR 2 Moderately followed	11	.086	1.135	1.685
RCR 3 Lightly followed	4	.101	1.209	1.822

Source: Steven Carvell and Paul Strebel, "A New Beta Incorporating Analysts Forecasts," *Journal of Portfolio Management*, Fall 1984. Reprinted with permission.

from the spotlight into the shadows, the systematic risk estimate increases dramatically when shadow risk is included.

In addition, the new beta was tested for its ability to explain monthly stock returns and for the extent to which it can account for the neglected firm effect. The new beta was found to be statistically superior to the historical beta in explaining monthly returns in the shadows. When used to risk-adjust the returns on the highly researched portfolios in the information spotlight, it had little impact on the returns, but reduced the excess returns in the shadows to zero. The implication is that the new beta risk adjusts the apparently abnormal returns on neglected stocks, where the historical beta fails to do so. The new beta, therefore, provides a much more accurate assessment of the systematic risk to which investors are exposed in the shadows.

SHADOW DIVERSIFICATION

Modern portfolio theory would suggest that risk assessment in the shadows would end with estimation of the new beta. The assumption is that portfolios can be formed that will diversify away all company specific risk. However, in the shadows, the picture is not so simple.

In contrast to the situation in the spotlight, company-specific risk cannot be easily diversified away in the shadows. The more narrowly focused the portfolio, the less the chance of finding stocks with offsetting company-related risk and, hence, the more restricted the maximum possible diversification. Stocks from the shadows often belong to firms in the same industries or sectors of the economy. For example, many small neglected firms come either from highly competitive industries with small economies of scale, or from new high-technology industries that have just been launched.

In addition, small neglected firms generally have greater total variability in their returns than those large firms, partly because they concentrate on narrower product lines. The lack of internal product line diversification causes greater company-specific risk. When this is added to the shadow danger of systematic extrapolation risk, it is not surprising that diversification possibilities are more limited in the shadows. Greater company-specific risk plus greater correlation between the returns on small neglected firms makes diversification in the shadows doubly difficult.

In the spotlight, it is well-known that one needs only 15 to 20 stocks in a portfolio to eliminate most of the diversifiable, unsystematic risk. But as shown in Figure 5.1, it may require ten times more securities in the shadows, up to 150 to 200 stocks, to get rid of the historically observed firm-specific risk. Even then, the residual portfolio risk of 0.073 is greater than the total risk of 0.065 for a single diversified large corporation in the spotlight. No matter how large the shadow portfolio, if the investor or manager restricts diversification to smaller firms in the shadows, the risk exposure is greater than that associated with investment in a single large company. For a portfolio comprising stocks from both the spotlight and the shadows, an intermediate number of securities is needed to obtain full diversification.

Since company-specific risk cannot be easily diversified away in the shadows, it cannot be so readily ignored as in the spotlight. This is especially true, because company-specific risk in the shadows frequently manifests itself in the form of greater bankruptcy risk. To prevent major losses in an investment portfolio by the inclusion of neglected stocks with hidden bankruptcy risk, assessment of the latter is imperative in the shadows.

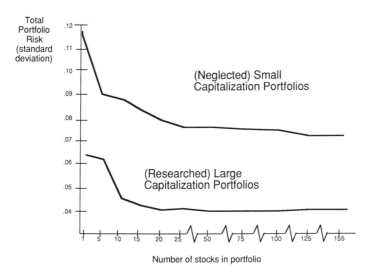

Figure 5.1 Impact of diversification on total risk.

BANKRUPTCY RISK

The possibility of bankruptcy is very real for neglected firms in the shadows. Despite important exceptions, many neglected firms are small and young. Of all the companies which went bankrupt in the United States in 1975, for example, 65.6 percent had a size, measured by the dollar value of liabilities, of less than $100,000, 30.3 percent a size of between $100,000 and $1 million, and only 4.1 percent a size greater than $1 million. The same Dun & Bradstreet survey found that 46.4 percent of the 1975 failures had been in existence for four years or less. It follows that firms in the shadows may be neglected precisely because of terminally poor performance. To avoid selecting these lemons, they must be identified.

Bankruptcy Ratios

Quantitative assessments of bankruptcy risk can be estimated. Perhaps the best-known are the financial ratio approaches—in particular, Altman's Z-score model. The Z-score is a weighted average of five ratios representing liquidity, profitability, leverage, solvency, and activity. The weights are obtained by comparing samples of bankrupt and nonbankrupt firms one or more years prior to bankruptcy and statistically selecting that combination of ratios which results in the cleanest Z-score-cut between the two types of firm. Companies with a Z-score below the cutoff point are regarded as safe, while those above the cutoff point are regarded as likely to go bankrupt. As an example of discriminating power, in the sample of 66 firms which Altman used to estimate the cutoff point, the total misclassification rate was five percent.

Other bankruptcy analysts have used essentially the same methodology, although with different ratios, samples, and time periods. The problem with all of these is that no one set of ratios and weights has emerged as universally successful at detecting bankruptcy, across industries and time periods. Owing to the absence of a rigorous theory of bankruptcy, it is impossible to select the ratios and weights from theoretical considerations. Empirically, the optimal weights vary with the sample and period. This is hardly surprising, because the weights and bankruptcy cutoff point during a recession will tend to be quite different from that obtained from a boom period.

To avoid having to reestimate the Z-score cutoff point, which is no simple task due to the data collection required, it is simpler and probably not much less accurate to use single ratios with cutoff points derived from the prevailing economic conditions. When comparing the performance of various models, Beaver found that single ratios often provide more accurate bankruptcy predictions than the more complex multiratio models.

The best performing single ratios were cash flow to total debt and net income to total assets. In Beaver's sample of 79 firms the total misclassification percentage was 13 percent for both ratios one year prior to bankruptcy and still less than 30 percent five years prior, which was superior to the Z-score percentage five years out in Altman's sample. Other related ratios, such as interest coverage or the debt service ratio, are less successful at bankruptcy prediction.

Of the two better performing ratios, cash flow to total debt reflects the ability of the company to repay its outstanding liabilities in the absence of refinancing. Cash flow represents annual funds from operations, or approximately net profits plus depreciation. Total debt includes all liabilities excluding net worth, that is, long- and short-term borrowings plus current liabilities. By including both current liabilities, usually financed by current assets, and short-term borrowings, often rolled over by the banks, the ratio represents a pessimistic appraisal of a company's financial position. However, as a means of detecting bankruptcy potential, this is quite appropriate. Companies threatened by bankruptcy often factor their accounts receivable and extend their overdraft facility, thereby severely limiting the refinancing of short-term borrowings. Without refinancing, a company with a cash-flow-to-total-debt ratio of .333, for example, could pay back its liabilities within an average period of three years. The appropriate cutoff point, therefore, depends on the average term of the company's debt. Clearly, the cash flow to total debt position should be comfortably above the maximum annual percentage repayments.

The return on assets, computed as the ratio of net income before interest to total assets, captures the company's operating performance. When compared to the cost of the firm's debt, it provides a critical reference for the transition point between a positive and negative leverage effect. If the return on assets drops below the interest rate, any debt in the capital structure pushes the return on equity downwards rather than upwards, because servicing the debt consumes more funds than an equivalent amount of equity. If the return on assets is measured after taxes, the appropriate comparison is the interest rate after taxes; if measured before taxes, it must be compared to the before-tax interest rate. In either case, the closer the return on assets to the prevailing interest rate, the greater the chance of a negative leverage effect and the greater the risk of bankruptcy.

Application of Bankruptcy Ratios

To illustrate the application of these ratios, let us consider the position of three computer companies, Apple, Commodore, and Wang, during a period when they were on the periphery of the shadows. We have selected these relatively well-known firms, rather than more neglected ones, to make it easier to place the examples in their environmental context, especially, during the qualitative discussion of company specific risk later on. Estimates of the cash flow to total debt and the return on assets after taxes and interest for the years 1978 to 1980 are shown in Table 5.4. The return on assets is computed after interest, due to the unavailability of data on interest payments for all three companies; this results in a conservative comparison with the interest rate. For all three companies, the return on assets, even when calculated after interest, was at least double the after-tax cost of interest of about 5 percent during the period, suggesting very low bankruptcy risk.

TABLE 5.4   Bankruptcy Predictors

	Apple	Commodore	Wang
Cash Flow/Total Debt			
1978	—	34.4%	31.5%
1979	115%	48.9	30.3
1980	145	31.5	28.4
Return on Assets			
1978	35.1%	20.9%	13.5%
1979	51.3	24.0	14.2
1980	44.4	30.0	14.5

Source: Annual Reports of Apple, Commodore, and Wang, 1978, 1979, 1980.

This conclusion is reinforced by the cash flow to total debt ratio. For Apple, the ratio was in excess of 100 percent. Apple had sufficient annual cash flow to repay all its liabilities in one year, if necessary. Commodore's ratio of around 30 percent in 1980 implies it could have liquidated all its liabilities within three years if necessary, without drawing on any funds other than its cash flow. Inspection of the notes to the annual report suggests an average liability maturity of just under five years, suggesting extremely low bankruptcy risk. Wang's ratio dropped below 30 percent in 1980, but the apparent average term of its liabilities was well over 10 years, also indicating virtually no risk of bankruptcy.

The level of a bankruptcy ratio at a single point in time, however, may be less important than its recent history. Argenti argues that there are common earnings trajectories which precede bankruptcy: "New companies" are often barely able to realize positive earnings before they disappear into bankruptcy; "show biz" companies, with a high news media profile, frequently exhibit rapidly rising earnings followed by a sudden even more dramatic collapse; "mature companies" exhibit flat earnings which drop to a lower plateau when the company loses its competitive edge, before ultimately failing. Although these earnings trajectories are largely impressionistic, the underlying idea is that the appropriate margin of safety above the reference point for a bankruptcy ratio depends on the variability in the company's earnings. This should include fluctuations due to both company-specific factors, as well as externally induced systematic risk.

In the case of Apple, Wang, and Commodore, the externally induced systematic risk was high. In addition to the bankruptcy predictors, Table 5.5 lists the number of analysts following the companies in 1980, as well as the coefficient of variation or spread in their forecasts, the historical beta, and the new beta. Apple, on the point of being listed, had no analyst coverage. Commodore with four analysts was lightly followed, while Wang with 13 analysts was moderately followed. The uncertainty in the analysts' forecasts, reflected in the coefficient of variation, increased as one moved into the shadows, from the moderately followed Wang to the lightly covered Commodore. The already high historical betas combined with this measure shadow of risk resulted in new betas of 2.2. Although the new beta could not be computed for Apple, owning to the absence of analysts' forecasts, it is safe to assume that,

TABLE 5.5 Systematic Shadow Risk and Bankruptcy Predictors

Companies 1980	No. of Analysts	Coefficient Variation	Historical Beta	New Beta	Cash Flow to Total Debt	Return on Assets
Wang	13	.084	1.65	2.2	28.4%	14.5%
Commodore	4	.103	1.60	2.2	31.5	30.0
Apple	0	N/A	1.80	N/A	145.0	44.4

N/A: not available due to lack of analyst coverage

Source: Adapted from I/B/E/S data. The Institutional Brokers Estimate System published by Lynch, Jones & Ryan, N.Y.C. Reprinted with permission.

as a more neglected stock, Apple had even higher implicit shadow risk.

For bankruptcy prediction, the high systematic risk injects a note of caution into the apparently safe levels of the bankruptcy ratios for the three companies listed in Table 5.5. Sharp environmental fluctuations, in the demand for computer products for example, would have been more than doubly magnified by the high systematic risk onto the return and price performance of the three stocks. Albeit somewhat remote in 1980, this danger was most significant for Wang, owning to the lower levels of its bankruptcy ratios.

Unfortunately, there is no combination of ratios that can fully capture company-specific and bankruptcy risk. This is especially so in the shadows, owning to the complex nature of shadow risk. A complete assessment of bankruptcy risk requires that quantitative ratio analysis be supplemented by qualitative, in-depth company analysis.

COMPANY ANALYSIS

The characteristics of a healthy company provide a reference framework for exposing the potential random threats to a firm and, hence, the hidden company-specific risk of the stock. While much of the necessary information for a thorough audit of the company may be difficult to obtain in the shadows, dangerous symptoms can often be picked up in the form of deviations from what are generally regarded as the norms of corporate health. For normative company analysis, the Japanese have a framework that considers the firm in terms of three interlocking inputs: personnel, money, and machines, or in more formal economic terms, labor, capital, and technology. To these, we add management strategy, which coordinates the inputs to the firm and targets its output.

Labor

The first of the three company inputs, the human system, is a frequently cited cause of corporate failure. As Argenti has pointed out, the underlying reason most often is lack of sensitivity to a changing environment. Among the telltale signs of such insensitivity are the following: autocratic one-person rule, which often leads to the kind of management myopia that makes adaptation to a changing environment virtually impossible; an inactive corporate board, or absence of external input to management, without which management can easily become too caught up in day-to-day business; the absence of managerial depth, especially in smaller firms, which may result in everything's depending on the original entrepreneur, or a key technical specialist, whose departure could disrupt the organization fatally.

A key test of the human system is its ability to adapt to a changing environment. For ongoing adaptation to an evolving industry environment, Lawrence and Dyer have argued that efficiency and innovation are key. The evolution of corporate organization can be described in terms of changes over time along the two dimensions of efficiency and innovation. Very briefly, the evolutionary process commences with highly innovative, organic management of the garage type, which characterized Apple's early days. In this kind of organization, control is exerted through peer group pressure, there are few formal systems, and efficiency is low. If the company survives its formative years and can make the transition to a more professional organization with the founding entrepreneur still in place, it is often very competitive, because while maintaining the entrepreneurial drive and vision of the founder, it has acquired the coordination systems needed for increased efficiency. When the founding entrepreneur passes away, the transition requires a replacement for the founder's vision. In many cases, this has turned out to be additional systems, which results in a mechanistic management style. Although improving efficiency somewhat, mechanistic management invariably stifles innovation. Finally, in the bureaucratic stages of organizational evolution, even efficiency atrophies, as control becomes more political in nature. This last type of organization is viable only in sheltered government or monopoly environments.

Look at our three computer companies: Apple could be classified in 1980 as struggling to make the transition from an innovative organic organization to a more professional, competitive firm. Although internally flexible, it was not very open to the environment, being guilty of a "not invented here" syndrome. (The annual reports reflect an entrepreneurial obsession for internal creativity and originality.) Wang was more clearly a competitive organization with a professional management, headed up by the original entrepreneur (Wang's reports contain numerous indicators of typical paternalistic concern for the employees' well-being) and a corresponding balance between innovation and efficiency. Commodore, by contrast, with its legal headquarters in the Bahamas, and a more faceless and less stable management, showed signs of being between a professional and a mechanistically oriented approach. (The annual reports contain little on the people in the company.)

As part of the assessment of company specific risk, which of the three companies was safest in terms of internal organizational cohesion and adaptability? Here we must take the industry environment into account, which will be done in Chapter 6. At this point, suffice it to say that in its emergence phase, the industry favored innovative companies, but, as the products began to diffuse through the market, attention to the market's needs became increasingly important. The vision and people-oriented philosophy of Dr. Wang suggest that his company was internally probably the most stable, as well as being externally the most adaptive, owing to the close attention paid to the customer's needs. Apple, by contrast, with its intermediate culture, between entrepreneuralism and professionalism, and relative insensitivity to market trends, exhibited the highest latent organizational risk of the three. Commodore's market orientation but more mechanistic management style probably placed it in the middle.

Technology

Evaluation of the second input, the company's technology, also requires a good dose of judgment and inference. Technology refers to all the activities of the company from R&D and design through purchasing, production, selling, distribution, and service. Very briefly again, the basic requirement is that the technology support the company's strategy. On the manufacturing side, when the strategy is oriented toward efficiency, desirable attributes include low inventories and little idle capacity. By contrast, when the strategy is innovation-oriented, manufacturing flexibility becomes critical. Product quality and labor productivity, as reflected in indicators like a low reject rate and high worker morale, are other signs of a healthy manufacturing operation. On the marketing side, market share and the growth rate are important indicators of whether the company's products have a viable market. Consistency within the marketing mix is also important. As emphasized by Peters and Waterman, most critical of all and a key characteristic of most successful companies is their strong sensitivity to overall market trends and especially to the customer.

The concentration of critical technological resources in a single supplier, or of experience in a single powerful group, creates a source of high risk. Raw materials from one supplier or experienced labor from a single union may be as risky on the technology input side as a single dominant product or narrow market segment on the output side. The same goes for dependence on government research, with defense contracts being notoriously exposed to the vagaries of shifting government policies.

On the basis of the annual reports, plus the little general information available, it was difficult to distinguish between the three computer companies in terms of their manufacturing and marketing technology. All that can be said is that, consistent with their declared strategies, Commodore was probably the most process-oriented, in its pursuit of the low-delivered-cost home market. Apple and Wang were probably more product- than process-oriented. With respect to marketing technology, Commodore and Wang seemed to have a clearer idea than Apple of the markets they were pursuing. But all three companies were segment leaders with very high growth rates in 1980 and no apparent sign that there might be any unpleasant surprises due to company-specific, technology-related factors.

Capital

The third company input, involving the financial system, is another frequently cited cause of corporate collapse. More specifically, the basic accounting information may be partially or even totally inadequate. Costing system weaknesses, poor budgeting control, or the absence of cash flow forecasting may all play a role in obscuring the basic financial health of the company, not to mention the sources of profitability and loss within its business mix.

Sometimes there is one big project that is too large for the company to absorb, either organizationally if the project succeeds, or financially if it fails. A rapid growth may also precipitate bankruptcy, if it inflates working and fixed capital requirements without being offset by new sources of financing.

In the face of excessive business risks, or financial risk in the form of high leverage, financing sources tend to dry up, making it impossible to meet existing contractual commitments. Especially ominous is any indication of creative accounting's being employed to cover up the true state of affairs. This is invariably a sign that management is preparing its own lifeboat while the ship is sinking. With respect to the three computer companies, the previous ratio analysis in Table 5.5 provided a partial assessment of the company-specific risk inherent in their financial subsystems.

Strategy

Strategy evaluation, the final component of company analysis, revolves around the fit between the core skills on which the company builds its product lines and the opportunities in the marketplace. To try and identify possible sources of company-specific risk, consider the dimensions of special expertise, which should set the company apart from the competition; second, the manner in which the firm's distinctive competence shapes its strategy; and third, the fit with the market opportunities.

A firm's sense of its own expertise can often be found between the lines in the general comments of the annual report. Although the interpretation of the comments is more of an art than a science, top management's view of the company's expertise usually stands out clearly, especially when reports are compared across companies in the same industry. As suggested earlier, the Apple Computer reports in the early 1980s continually celebrated the company's innovative abilities, both in product design and manufacture, although its market focus came through much less clearly. Commodore International, by contrast, emphasized its low-cost products aimed at the home market. Wang Laboratories, on the other hand, stressed the ability to innovate for, and adapt to, evolving customer preferences in the office automation market.

Another indication of a company's core skills is implicit in the way it actually combines industry activities vertically, or product lines and markets horizontally. Thus, Apple's innovative emphasis was manifest in its organization around new product development teams, aimed at coming up with state-of-the-art, quality, user-friendly PCs. Commodore's vertically integrated manufacturing and geographically organized marketing was the basis of its focus on the high-volume, low-cost home market. Wang organized its business, not so much around technology, although this was important for all companies in the industry, but around units serving the office information market.

Given a sense of the company's distinctive competence, how does it shape the strategy? Here the key indicator is provided by the allocation of capital expenditure. The firm's investment decisions can be regarded as the most direct manifestation of its strategy. Although the magnitude of capital expenditure is in the annual report, its composition is usually only hinted at in qualitative terms. Additional information of this type can be very valuable in the shadows, but is extremely difficult to get. In the case of the three computer companies, as far as one can tell from the annual reports, their capital expenditure programs were apparently designed to capitalize on and reinforce their perceived strength.

There remains the third and crucial strategic question of whether the investment objectives are consistent with the opportunities revealed by industry analysis (see Chapter 6). Has the company been able to identify market opportunities for exploiting its expertise and thereby to create financial value? Or is the strategy out of touch with the industry environment?

All three computer companies under discussion were in rapidly emerging markets in 1980. The importance of product development in the emerging 1980 personal computer industry made Apple's strategy apparently well suited to the industry environment of the time. Commodore's attempt to standardize the home computer was a bold and correspondingly risky move in the face of a still rapidly evolving product, although, if successful, standardization would have permitted Commodore to outpace the competition. Wang's market-driven approach to the development of office equipment was particularly well suited to its market segment which reflected office-based end-users. The one sign of company-specific risk connected to strategy was Commodore's attempt to standardize the home computer, which might have been regarded as premature in 1980.

In brief, the high systematic risk of the three companies (see Table 5.5) was compounded in the case of Wang by a somewhat looser safety net than was possibly needed, reflected in the lower bankruptcy predictors; in the case of Apple, organizational fragility compounded the high systematic risk, while in the case of Commodore it was potentially misdirected strategy.

It follows from the discussion in this chapter that risk management in the shadows must differ from that in the spotlight on two counts. First, the potential for diversification is limited in the shadows, and company-specific risk plays a correspondingly more important role. Thus, it is essential that company-specific risk be assessed. To remove company-specific risk full diversification requires incorporation of the shadow portfolio into a larger portfolio, a topic considered in Chapter 10. When full diversification is not possible, high company-specific risk may require the elimination of individual stocks from further consideration (see Chapter 9).

Second, systematic risk in the shadows tends to be much greater than in the spotlight. Since this risk cannot be diversified away, it must be balanced by a correspondingly high return potential. Evaluation of the latter is pursued in Chapter 6.

APPENDIX TO CHAPTER 5

This appendix presents a simplified outline of the derivation of the new beta. For more detail, see Strebel (1983).

In the presence of uncertainty in the mean of a return distribution, the total risk (σ_τ^2) faced by investors can be shown to be the sum of the historical variance in returns (σ_h^2) plus the variance in the mean $(\sigma_\ast^2)$:

$$\sigma_\tau^2 = \sigma_h^2 + \sigma_\ast^2 \qquad (1)$$

The variance in the mean can be estimated from the historical standard error in the mean (σ_h^2/T), where T is the number of observations in the historical time series sample of returns, and from the variance between the analysts' forecasts of the mean return (σ_a^2):

$$\sigma_*^2 = [T/\sigma_h^2 + 1/\sigma_a^2]^{-1} \qquad (2)$$

Substitution of Eq. (2) in Eq. (1) yields the total risk faced by investors, which can be incorporated into the CAPM or a single-factor generating model to obtain a new beta that includes the impact of uncertainty in the mean of the return distribution:

$$\beta_{\text{New}} = \rho\sigma_r/\sigma_m$$

$$\beta_{\text{New}} = (\rho/\sigma_m)\{\sigma_h^2 + [T/\sigma_h^2 + 1/\sigma_a^2]^{-1}\}^{1/2}$$

$$\beta_{\text{New}} = \{(\rho^2\sigma_h^2/\sigma_m^2) + (\rho^2/\sigma_m^2)[T/\sigma_h^2 + 1/\sigma_a^2]^{-1}\}^{1/2}$$

$$\beta_{\text{New}} = \{\beta^2{}_{\text{historical}} + \beta^2{}_{\text{shadow risk}}\}^{1/2}$$

where ρ is the correlation between the security and market returns and σ_m is the variance in the market returns.

A key assumption is that the instability in the mean is indeed correlated with the market and that the historical correlation coefficient provides a reasonable representation of this dependence. The reasoning is that we are not dealing with estimation risk generated by forecasting errors on the part of investors, which can be diversified away. Rather, the new beta reflects systematic shadow risk caused by jumps in the environment and the extrapolation from the spotlight into the shadows.

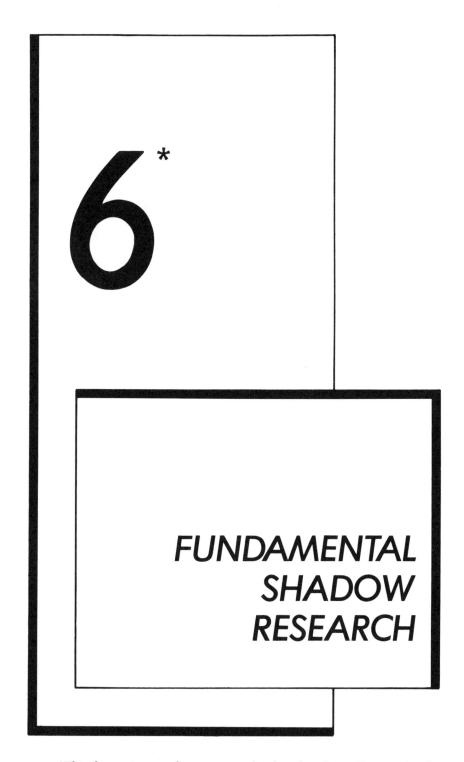

6*

FUNDAMENTAL SHADOW RESEARCH

*This chapter is somewhat more complex than the others. Those not familiar with the use of valuation methods in the spotlight may merely want to skim this material on a first reading, so as not to lose the flow of ideas.

What is a neglected stock worth? Given its risk, is it selling at a discount relative to its intrinsic value? This chapter is concerned with the fundamental research required to assess the value of a company in order to determine whether a neglected stock is also a discount stock. For the shadows, the most appropriate valuation methods are those which are sufficiently flexible to permit the incorporation of quantitative and qualitative information. The chapter introduces a flexible valuation model and discusses its application to the shadows. A qualitative approach to industry and competitive analysis is outlined. It is shown how discount stocks can be found by combining the industry and competitive fundamentals with the valuation model.

A VALUATION MODEL FOR THE SHADOWS

Piercing the shadows with the flashlight of fundamental research is never straightforward. It requires an intuitive mix of analysis and judgment that is tricky to implement owing to the paucity of shadow information. What is needed is a valuation framework that is sufficiently flexible to permit the use of what little information is available. The discrete growth valuation model introduced in this section is especially suited to this task. It makes the link between a firm's value and its strategy more transparent than most other models, thereby facilitating different combinations of quantitative and qualitative analysis. As an introduction to the discrete growth model, a very brief review of valuation methods is appropriate.

Liquidation versus Ongoing Firm Valuation

Despite the multiplicity of approaches to valuation, most fall into one of two basic categories: the liquidation approach, which asks how much the company would be worth if it were liquidated; and the ongoing firm approach, which estimates its value as an ongoing entity. For shadow investment purposes, the liquidation method is most relevant when the balance sheet includes large underutilized assets that make the company potentially more valuable as a liquidated rather than as a continuing operation. When this is the case, the company's stock would be selling at a discount, if based on the ongoing value, rather than the potential liquidation value.

Neglected stocks in this category are indeed discount stocks, with the discount equal to the difference between the two values.

Since underutilized assets often attract takeovers, the liquidation framework may be used to pick potential takeover candidates. However, the probability of identifying underutilized assets is much lower in the shadows. Information on the true value of balance sheet assets is often difficult to obtain. As a result, the application of the liquidation method in the shadows is very dependent on access to institutional information regarding the probability of a takeover and is not considered further here.

The vast majority of neglected stocks are worth more as ongoing entities. Apart from the company's market price, the overall methods for evaluating ongoing firms involve either ratio comparisons with other companies or attempts to put a value on the company's projected cash flow stream. The comparisons, based on the ratio of price to earnings, dividends, cash flow, or other variables, are difficult to apply with precision. Very few companies are similar enough to make the ratio for one appropriate to another. In particular, the application of a spotlight ratio to a neglected stock in the shadows is of questionable value.

Adjustments to make the ratios more comparable depend on an understanding of how the underlying variables affect prices. For this, it is necessary to get to the heart of cash flow valuation. The key ingredient is some kind of long-run cash flow projection. But cash flows are not easy to forecast—hence the tendency to fall back on simplifying assumptions. In mature industries, for example, it may be reasonable to assume that the cash flow will remain more or less constant, or will grow slowly at a constant rate into the foreseeable future. These common assumptions are not so realistic when companies are small, or in rapid expansion, often the situation for interesting firms coming out of the shadows.

Discrete Growth Model

A much more useful approach, put forward by Modigliani and Miller, is to base the cash flow projection on discrete growth opportunities and then to segment the valuation procedure into two pieces: first, an estimate of the value generated by investments already made, that is, the value of the existing cash flow stream; second, an estimate of the value associated with future investment or growth opportunities. The modified formulas needed to calculate the current earnings and future growth values are shown in Table 6.1 and discussed below.

The value of the existing cash flow stream can be easily obtained by regarding it as a constant annuity. Often it may be assumed that depreciation more or less covers investment in maintenance, so that the net cash flow from the business in place can be approximated by net earnings. The value of the existing cash flow stream is then given by net earnings divided by the opportunity cost of the shareholders funds. (NPAT/K in Table 6.1). Thus, for a company with continuing net profits after tax of $1.2 million, say, and

TABLE 6.1   Discrete Growth Model

V_T		V_0		V_G
Total value	$=$	Current earnings value	$+$	Future growth value

V_G		Growth quality		Growth quantity
Future growth value	$=$	Value associated with each dollar of new investment	$\times$	Total future investment in present value dollars

Current earnings value	$=$	$\dfrac{\text{Current earnings}}{\text{Cost of equity}}$	$=$	$\dfrac{\text{NPAT}}{\text{K}}$
Growth quality	$=$	$\dfrac{\text{Return on equity} \times 1}{\text{Cost of equity}} - 1 =$		$\left[\dfrac{R}{K} - 1\right]$
Growth quantity	$=$	Present value of future investment stream	$=$	$PV(I)$

$$V_T = \frac{\text{NPAT}}{\text{K}} + \left[\frac{R}{K} - 1\right]^0 PV(I)$$

an opportunity cost of shareholder funds of 10 percent, the value of the current earnings stream would be $12 million.

The cost of equity or shareholder funds can be tricky to estimate. The most systematic approach is provided by the capital asset pricing model, developed by Sharpe, Lintner, and Mossin. The company's risk, and hence risk premium, is calculated relative to the premium for the stock market as a whole, using the historical beta coefficient, and then added to the yield on long-term government bonds. The risk premium for the market reflects the 50-year average difference in return (7 percent in the United States) between the market and long-term government bonds. Thus, a beta coefficient of 0.5, say, in an environment yielding 6.5 percent on long-term government bonds corresponds to a cost of equity estimate of $10\% = 6.5\% + (0.5) \times (7\%)$.

In the case of neglected firms, however, this historical approach ignores the high levels of uncertainty surrounding their future returns. The historical approach does not take account of the greater instability in the returns on neglected stocks. To cope with this problem, Chapter 5 introduced the new beta incorporating shadow risk. Whenever the variance in analysts' forecasts is available, the new beta should be used for valuation in the shadows. When not available, the best that can be done is to adjust the historical beta up, according to the stock's neglect classification, the relationship between new beta and neglect in Table 5.3 being used as a guide. At a minimum, if even the historical beta cannot be obtained, an intuitive estimate of the risk premium can be added to the long-term government bond rate.

As shown in Table 6.1, the value of future growth opportunities can be decomposed into the product between the growth quality, or value associated with each dollar of new investment, and the growth quantity, the total amount of anticipated future investment by the company. The growth quality is really the net present value generated by each dollar of new investment. If the anticipated return on new equity investment is $R = 24$ percent, say, then each dollar of investment will generate a $0.24 stream of profits, which at an opportunity cost of $K = 10$ percent, is worth $0.24/0.10 = $2.4. The growth quality, or net value created by the dollar investment, is therefore $(R/K - 1) = $2.4 - $1.0 = $1.4.

The quantity of growth reflects the anticipated investment stream that is likely to earn the return built into the growth quality. For example, if the 24 percent anticipated return on equity is associated with a five-year stream of $1 million equity investment per annum, the quantity of this growth is merely the present value of the five-year investment stream, $PV(I)$ = $1 million × present value annuity factor for 5 years at 10 percent = $1 million × 3.8 = $3.8 million. The value of future growth, the product of the quality and quantity, is then given by $(R/K - 1)$ × $PV(I)$ = 1.4 × $3.8 million = $5.3 million. Finally, the total estimated value of the company can be obtained from the sum of the current earnings value and the future growth value, which is equal to $12 million + $5.3 million = $17.3 million.

SHADOW APPLICATION OF THE DISCRETE GROWTH MODEL

The great advantage of the discrete growth model is that it can be adapted to the availability of information in the shadows. The discrete growth model is directly built up as the sum of the economic components of the business. In the shadows, pieces of the company are often much simpler to evaluate than the total future cash flows required by other valuation models.

In particular, it is usually possible to value current earnings in the shadows. The estimation of a current earnings value requires as data inputs net earnings and the cost of equity. The former is generally available, while the latter can be approximated by adding a risk premium to the prevailing government bond rate. Once a value has been obtained for current earnings, the value of future growth can be computed immediately by subtracting the earnings value from the total value of the firm. In Table 6.1, ($V_G = V_T - V_O$). The market's assessment of future potential is implicit in the proportion of the firm's value associated with future growth rather than current earnings. The ratio of growth value to earnings value thus can be used to infer the market's opinion about the firm's life cycle phase.

The implicit life cycle phase can then be compared with the

evolutionary phase of the industry and the competitive position of the firm as revealed by industry and competitive analysis. A company might be regarded as undervalued, for example, if the life cycle phase implicit in its market price suggests much less potential than that exposed by qualitative industry and competitive analysis.

After the life cycle phase has been assessed, a second objective of industry and competitive analysis is to understand how the neglected firms are competing, which of them is most likely to succeed, and hence how the companies are likely to perform qualitatively with respect to future return. The projected trend in future return extracted from industry and competitive analysis may be compared for valuation purposes, with the future return implicit in the neglected firm's stock price. The implicit future return can be obtained from the discrete growth model provided a growth estimate is available.

Thus, two shadow comparisons are feasible, between the life cycle phase and the future return implicit in the market price on the one hand, and the corresponding assessments generated by industry and competitive analysis on the other hand. As shown in Figure 6.1, this approach avoids the problem of valuing future growth and returns in the shadows, by turning these from inputs into outputs of the research process.

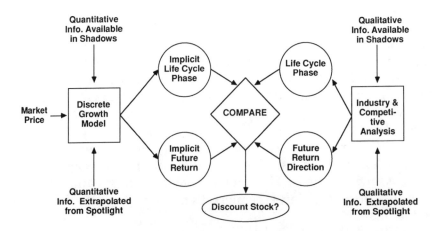

Figure 6.1   Approach to fundamental research in the shadows.

On the one side, the method involves using the discrete growth model to work backward from the market price to estimates of the implicit life cycle phase and future return. The necessary quantitative information reflects what is available in the shadows complemented by related information taken from the spotlight. There is no need to stick slavishly to life cycle and future returns as the outputs. Other outputs can be chosen to take advantage of whatever quantitative information is available in the shadows. On the other side, industry and competitive analysis can be employed with a mix of qualitative data from the shadows and spotlight, to generate qualitative opinions about the life cycle phase and direction of future returns. Comparison of the two sets of output permits an opinion to be formed on whether the neglected stock being researched is possibly a discount stock.

As an illustration, we shall outline the analysis for the computer industry in the early 1980s. This industry has the advantage of being well-known, making it simpler for the reader to fill in missing details and put the discussion into context. In addition, the early 1980s were a period of transition for the computer industry, characterized by the emergence of the personal computer. Since industries in transition are typically more complex to analyze, the principles of this example should be transferable to other industries in transition, as well as to more stable ones.

IMPLICIT LIFE CYCLE PHASE

As suggested above, comparison of the future growth value and the current earnings value permits an assessment of the market's opinion about the company's future potential and hence its implicit life cycle phase. Examination of the patterns associated with the different phases of industry evolution suggests the following loose classification scheme (Table 6.2): Growth value less than earnings value is typical of companies that the market perceives to be mature. Companies perceived to have viable differentiation strategies have growth values at least of the order of their earnings value. Rapidly growing companies, by comparison, have a future growth value

TABLE 6.2   Earnings (V_O) Versus Future Value (V_G)
and Implicit Life Cycle Phase

Relationship	Relative Growth Value (V_G/V_O)	Phase
$V_G < V_O$	< 1	Maturity
$V_G \approx V_O$	≈ 1	Differentiation
$V_G > V_O$	> 1	Growth
$V_G \gg V_O$	$\gg 1$	Emergence

that is significantly greater than fifty percent of their total value. Finally, for the leading companies in emerging industries, the value of growth opportunities comprises almost all of their value, especially when current earnings are small.

For companies in the shadows, obvious discrepancies between the market's assessment of the life cycle phase and that revealed by industry analysis are potential evidence that the firm's stock is selling at a discount. To illustrate how this comparison can be made, Table 6.3 lists 10 companies in the computer industry, with the number of analysts following them, the values of their current earnings and future growth, and the corresponding implicit life cycle phase at the end of 1980.

As an example, let us look at the case of Wang Labs at the end of 1980, after the emergence of the PC industry, but prior to the introduction of the IBM standard. The total value of Wang at the end of 1980 was \$2.04 billion based on 56 million shares outstanding at a price of \$36$\frac{3}{8}$. Wang's anticipated 1981 net earnings, reported in the Standard and Poors Earnings Forecaster of December 1980, were \$70.8 million. The opportunity cost of shareholders' equity capital, derived from the capital asset pricing model, was approximately 22.8 percent, reflecting a T-bond yield of 10.9 percent plus a risk premium of $1.7 \times 7\% = 11.9\%$, where 1.7 is Wang's beta coefficient and 7 percent is the market risk premium. The capitalized value of the existing earnings stream, therefore, was $V_O = $70.8/0.228 = 310 billion. The value attributed by the market to Wang's future growth opportunities was $V_G = $2.04 - $0.31 = 1.73 billion. With future growth opportunities valued at more than five times existing earnings, Wang was clearly regarded by the market as an emerging company.

Seven of the companies, with a following of more than 15 an-

TABLE 6.3   Implicit Life Cycle Phase: Computer Industry

Company 1980	No. of Analysts	Earnings Value (V_O) ($ millions)	Growth Value (V_G) ($ millions)	Relative Growth Value (V_G/V_O)	Implicit Life Cycle Phase
Apple	—	$ 51	$1400	27.30	Emergence
Burroughs	22	1449	787	.54	Mature
Commodore	4	82	417	5.05	Emergence
Control Data	16	788	516	.65	Mature
Data General	22	340	343	1.01	Differentiation
Digital	23	1673	3222	1.93	Growth
IBM	22	22772	16854	.74	Mature
NCR	17	1343	655	.49	Mature
Sperry	16	1721	895	.52	Mature
Wang	13	310	1733	5.59	Emergence

Source: Adapted from Paul Strebel, "The Stock Market and Competitive Analysis," *Strategic Management Journal,* Vol. 4, John Wiley and Sons, Ltd., 1983. Reprinted with permission.

alysts, could be classified as highly researched and well within the information spotlight. Since information is most available in the spotlight, one would expect the market prices of these companies to most closely reflect the industry fundamentals. Of the seven, five (IBM, Burroughs, Control Data, NCR, and Sperry) were implicitly valued as mature, one (Data General) was valued as if in a differentiation phase, and one (Digital) had a growth phase valuation.

As mentioned in Chapter 5, Wang, with between five and fifteen analysts, was moderately researched, that is, on the periphery of the information spotlight. Commodore, listed since the earlier nineteen-seventies, with four analysts in 1980, was further into the shadows with a small following. Apple, which only went public at the end of 1980, was not listed by I/B/E/S. Yet all three companies had very high relative growth values, suggesting that the market perceived them as emerging companies. To assess the reasonableness of the market's perception, let us turn to the picture generated by industry and competitive analysis.

INDUSTRY ANALYSIS

The activities of an industry comprise the whole vertical chain from raw material procurement through to final end product distribution and service. In the computer industry, competitors are not necessarily involved in all activities. One company might define itself as an upstream manufacturer, concentrating on the activities of making integrated circuits and other parts. A second company, like Apple, might concentrate on design, assembly, and marketing. A third, like Wang, might add distribution and customer service to its activities. A fourth might be vertically integrated, like IBM, competing in all the activities of the industry. In this case, the overlapping competitive patterns suggest that the industry be defined to include the whole chain of activities.

Although critical to corporate success, the activity chain may be difficult to pin down, especially in a rapidly evolving industry. Consider the problem of evaluating companies in the personal computer industry in the middle 1980s. Although still less than a decade old, the industry was already showing signs of maturity. After a little more than two years of great enthusiasm following the entry of the IBM PC, users were having second thoughts. The impossibility of communicating between machines of different makes and of reading data from mainframes was looking more and more like a real limitation. The future seemed to lie in integrated information systems and networks. Evaluating the potential of various manufacturers, the critical question was what industry they were in: personal computers, work stations, or integrated information systems? The only way of making a choice was in the dynamic context of the industry's evolution.

Evolution of Industries

Even though the detailed evolution of industries varies widely across technologies and markets, useful generalizations can be made about the shifts in competitive advantage that take place as an industry passes from one stage of its evolution to another. Schematically, the idealized evolution of an industry can be depicted as shown in Figure 6.2. The competitive dimensions associated with the different stages of industry evolution can be summarized as follows:

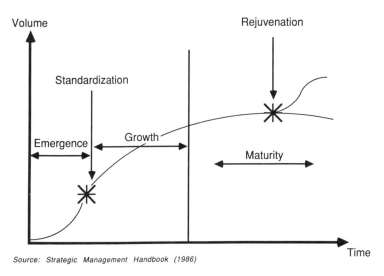

Source: Strategic Management Handbook (1986)

Figure 6.2   Industry evolution: An idealized representation.

1. Emergence: fundamental product development (usually tech-nology driven).
2. Standardization and market development: shift towards low-ering the delivered cost of the developed product through process improvement (usually cost driven).
3. Maturity and rejuvenation: shift towards product differentia-tion in addition to an efficient process (usually market driven).
4. Repetition of phases 2 and 3.

The number of times phases 2 and 3 might repeat themselves is impossible to predict. Some industries, like the various sectors of financial services, experience long periods of maturity after stand-ardization, before being shaken to the core by rejuvenation. In the case of financial services, the shake-up was initiated by deregula-tion and imported technology. In generating irresistible pressure for rejuvenation, external forces made it easier in the financial services industry to foresee the inevitability of an evolutionary transition.

Anticipating Industry Transitions

In most industries, it is more difficult to predict the evolu-tionary transitions. But prediction can be facilitated by scanning the industry environment for characteristic indicators. The reju-venation transition is usually preceded by one or both of the fol-lowing: declining returns to investment in further process improve-ment, often associated with slowing progress down the learning curve; increasing competitive stalemate, frequently accompanied by declining or negative growth rates. The standardization tran-sition may be preceded by: declining returns to investment in fur-ther fundamental development of the product, which is a sign of increasing stability in the underlying technology; the development of a market large enough to support standardization; increasing im-itation of the basic product, a sign of its growing market credibility.

In the PC industry of 1980, for example, the product had be-gun to stabilize, new entrants were imitating rather than innovat-ing, and the market had expanded significantly, all of which set the stage for impending standardization. By 1985, the IBM standard and its clones had further developed the market dramatically;

growth rates had begun to decline, leading to much greater competitive pressures, and little more could be squeezed out of the manufacturing and distribution process in term of efficiency, which in turn set the stage for the next act, rejuvenation.

For investors, rejuvenation marks a second key turning point in the fate of many companies, because it signals another realignment of the relevant competitive advantages. At the end of 1984 and in 1985, this occurred in the personal computer industry. IBM launched its PC-AT. Networks began to receive increasing attention from competitors like Digital Equipment. Resources were now channelled both to the process and to new product generation, such as integrated computer networks. These developments were in the hands of a few large competitors who could be active on both fronts, process and product, putting together the complete package. If we look ahead from 1985 in the PC industry, typical patterns of industry evolution suggest that, after network development, would come network standardization, which would be followed by market development and maturity, with the stage then set for a new round of rejuvenation.

In the context of the computer industry as a whole, it is clear that the PC was not so much a new industry as a rejuvenation transition within the continuing evolution of the larger industry. The PC was a form of sharp product differentiation that opened up large market segments hitherto ignored by the computer industry: professionals, small business, and non-specialist users in large organizations who wished to escape the power of the electronic data processing department. Prior to the personal computer, it was the minicomputer which had rejuvenated the industry, become standardized, and diffused through the market before developing signs of maturity. Before the mini, the industry went through repeated rounds of main frame development, based mainly on fundamental technological progress rather than market differentiation.

To summarize for the purposes of our example: in 1980, as we have seen, the computer industry was in the early stages of rejuvenation by the micro computer. The big question was which companies would be able to take advantage of the rejuvenation to boost their market position and which would be adversely affected and left behind. To assess the relative competitive advantage of the firms, let us examine the state of competition in the industry.

COMPETITIVE ANALYSIS

Only the very best of companies are able to combine the basic competitive thrusts of low delivered cost and superior product value. Then only for relatively short periods, until the competition catches up. Most companies are forced to make trade-offs between the two. A higher-value product normally necessitates greater production costs, while lower delivered cost usually requires the sacrifice of valuable features.

Value Cost Tradeoff

Consequently, the competitors in an industry can be positioned according to the trade-off they have made between perceived value and delivered cost. The resulting mapping can then be examined for signs of strategic groups of competitors who seem to be making a similar trade-off between value to the customer and process cost. The objective is to determine how the key competitors are obtaining their competitive advantage.

To proceed, let us return to the computer industry. Product value can be defined as the average dollar value per unit sold, that is, the average unit price. Process cost is then the pretax dollar cost per unit sold. In industries like automobiles the unit numbers can be taken out of the annual reports. But in many industries, computers included, unit sales are not readily available to outsiders. The fallback position is a subjective ranking of competitors based on a qualitative assessment of their strategies.

A qualitative mapping of the computer industry companies onto the price and cost axes is shown in Figure 6.3. The solid diagonal line is the zero profit per unit line. Performance is indicated by the vertical distance above and below this line, which measures profits and loss per unit, respectively.

The lowest cost unit sales reflect the simplest systems with the least complex software and related service. Apple can be positioned at this end of the market with its innovation in low-cost end-user computing. In 1980, Apple was benefiting from the high returns which successful innovators command. Its product was perceived to be of high value relative to its production cost, which resulted in a high profit margin. Hence its position well above the zero profit

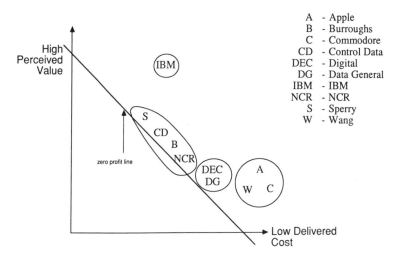

Figure 6.3   Perceived value—delivered cost trade-off computer industry 1980.

line. Next in delivered cost per unit was probably Wang, with its heavy emphasis on word processors. Wang, too, was still benefiting from the high returns to its innovation in office automation.

Further up the cost axis was the group of companies commonly referred to as the BUNCH—Burroughs, NCR, Control Data, Sperry—competitors with very much less clearly defined strategies and correspondingly poor performance. All were profitable in 1980, but with returns on the book value of equity well below the share holders' opportunity cost. By contrast, the leaders in the mini-computer segment, Digital Equipment and Data General, were earning very solid returns, a direct reflection of their competitive position. Finally, at the high-value end of the market, there was the overall leader, IBM. Despite its size, IBM still had high-quality growth with returns well above the cost of equity.

Figure 6.3 suggests at least four distinct strategic groups: First, the pioneers in the emerging and rapidly growing micro and word-processor segments. These companies were exploiting the high perceived value of their innovative low-cost products. Second, the leaders during the previous rejuvenation phase, the main mini manufacturers. Their objective was to maintain market share leadership of the mini segment by increasing efficiency. Third, the middle market companies with fuzzy strategies caught between the value and cost axes. And fourth, the overall market leader. IBM was the master of strategic switching between product value enhancement in the form of a new computer series and subsequent price reduction designed to keep the competitors at bay.

Competitive Scenario

The next step is to forecast the likely evolution of these strategic groups in the context of the industry dynamics discussed earlier and the related competitive pressure points and opportunities. The central question is which of the groups was likely to benefit the most, and conversely be hardest hit, by the development of the micro. How would they be affected by the micro as a potential substitute for their products and by the micro manufacturers as new entrants into the industry? Which of the groups could best capitalize on the shifting mix of supplier, customer, and competitive pressures? At the company level, how did they compare in terms of their ability to develop a competitive formula for dealing with, even better exploiting, the thrust towards low-cost, user-friendly computing?

The companies most likely to be affected technologically were those closest to lower-cost, user-friendly computing: the mini manufacturers, Digital and Data General, and companies like Burroughs and NCR. If able to follow quickly, they might have been able to turn the micro to their advantage by exploiting existing marketing and distribution systems. But their strategies were not conducive to incorporation of the unorthodox micro. By the end of 1980, these firms showed no signs of even having appreciated the significance of the micro. Thus, the most probable outcome was downward pressure on their return performance.

The same conclusion was reasonable for Sperry and Control Data, although of lesser magnitude, because of greater distance from the low-cost end-user segments. Even IBM was likely to come under pressure as the cutting edge of product market growth shifted from the large computer segment, where IBM was dominant, towards micro computers and new user-friendly software, where IBM had yet to display any observable interest. (At the time, there were no signs that IBM would be able or willing to alter its traditional methods to accommodate the open architecture, subcontracted software, and indirect distribution associated with the micro.) In the case of Wang, the outcome was very uncertain. Would the micro invade its market, or could it convert the word processor into a more general-purpose micro?

Among the neglected firms, the strategies of Apple and Commodore were focused directly on the emerging opportunity. The issue was whether they could maintain their high returns in the face of the low barriers to entry. And which of the two would emerge with the industry standard, the higher-quality Apple, or the lower-cost Commodore? Overall, among the neglected firms, those most likely to benefit were the hardier competitors among the hundreds of unknown imitators flooding into the market.

At this point a comparison can be made with the life cycle phases implicit in the companies' market values (Table 6.3). The competitive scenario implied declining returns for Burroughs, Control Data, NCR, and Sperry, probably also for Digital and Data General, with relatively constant returns for IBM, and uncertain returns for Wang, Apple, and Commodore. This assessment is consistent with the market's classification of Burroughs, Control Data, NCR, Sperry, and IBM as mature. It suggests that the valuations of Digital and Data General as growth and differentation types, respectively, might have been somewhat optimistic.

Of the peripheral shadow firms, Wang's very high relative growth value in Table 6.3 was consistent with its leading position in the rapidly expanding word processor market, but perhaps overly optimistic given the uncertainty of its response to the micro. Apple also seemed to be fully priced with an extremely high relative growth value given the uncertainty about its future returns level. Compared to Apple, Commodore's growth value was more modest but in the same relative range as Wang's.

IMPLICIT FUTURE RETURN

To get the future return out of the discrete growth model, values are required for the other variables in Table 6.1. In particular, an estimate is needed of the growth quantity. One way of estimating the anticipated growth quantity is to assume that it is proportional to the current equity growth rate, with a proportionality coefficient corresponding to the present value time profile of future investment.

To illustrate the approach, we shall assume that the same present value factor can be used for all ten companies in the sample, because they were exposed to a similar time profile of industry growth opportunities. The approximate magnitude of the factor can be calculated from the discrete growth model by using one company as a reference point and assuming that its future return can be approximated by its current return. Owing to the relative stability of IBM's return, it provided the obvious reference point in the computer sample.

IBM's current 1980 return on equity was 24 percent. With a cost of equity of 17 percent, this corresponds to a growth quality of $Q = .24/.17 - 1 = .41$. The value of IBM's future growth was previously calculated to be $V_G = \$16.8$ billion (Table 6.3). In the context of the discrete growth model, the growth quantity G is equal to the growth value V_G divided by the growth quality Q; $G = V_G/Q = \$40.9$ billion. The present value factor (PVF) can then be estimated from the growth quantity divided by the five-year equity growth rate up to 1980 of 11.1 percent, times the 1980 equity base of \$16.4 billion, $PVF = 40.9/(0.111 \times 16.4) = 22.4$, or approximately $PVF = 20$.

Given the present value factor of $PVF = 20$ plus five-year equity growth rates, and the equity bases, the quantities of growth can be obtained for the other companies. The future return on equity follows by substituting the quantity of growth into the discrete growth model. The results are shown in Table 6.4.

Assuming a present value factor of 20, the market seems to have been valuing the more mature companies using a common industry-wide future return on equity of around 24 percent. The market was apparently unable to discriminate between the mature companies on the basis of potential future return. Rather than reflecting differing future returns, the valuation differences seem to have been based on more readily available differences in current earnings and growth rate data.

Whatever the case, the market seemed to anticipate an increasing return trend for these companies, which contradicts the perspective revealed by industry and competitive analysis, especially for the companies in the middle-market strategic group: Bur-

TABLE 6.4   Implicit Future Return on Equity:
Computer Industry

Company 1980	Equity Growth Rate	Cost of Equity	Current Return on Equity	Implicit Future Return on Equity
Apple	167.0%	22.8%	45.2%	59.5%
Burroughs	6.1	17.9	12.2	23.3
Commodore	70.0	20.5	47.6	37.5
Control Data	10.1	22.0	11.9	25.9
Data General	18.0	19.0	20.2	24.7
Digital	17.5	19.4	19.7	30.2
Honeywell	11.4	19.8	13.9	24.8
IBM	11.1	17.1	23.7	24.0
NCR	9.3	20.1	15.8	24.2
Sperry	5.7	19.0	14.0	25.5
Wang	62.0	22.8	37.0	37.5

Source: Adapted from Paul Strebel, "The Stock Market and Competitive Analysis," *Strategic Management Journal*, Vol. 4, John Wiley and Sons, Ltd., 1983. Reprinted with permission.

roughs, Control Data, NCR, and Sperry. As we have seen, there was little in the fundamentals to suggest that their currently poor returns, below the cost of equity, would improve toward the level of the market leaders. Rather than being discount stocks, if anything, the implicit future return analysis suggests that these companies were optimistically valued.

Expecting IBM and Wang to maintain their return levels was not inconsistent with the fundamentals. On the other hand, the relatively sharp increases in implicit return for Digital and to a lesser extent, Data General, were optimistic in the light of their possible exposure to the microcomputer. Perhaps the market was expecting them to mount the micro bandwagon. Whatever the case, these two were certainly not undervalued.

The one company which stood out in 1980 was Commodore, valued by the market with a declining return trend: a future return on equity of 37.5 percent versus a current return of 47.6 percent. This was especially noteworthy in contrast to the optimism surrounding Apple when it went public, reflected in the company's implicitly rising return trend. Looking back at the company analysis in Chapter 5, as well as the industry and competitive analysis of this chapter, we see that there was little in the two firms' risk or growth opportunities to explain the difference. Taking the analysis so far, as a whole therefore, and comparing the two, we can say that Commodore could be classified tentatively as a discount stock relative to Apple.

IMPLICATIONS FOR SECURITY RESEARCH

The approach to fundamental shadow research outlined in this chapter is heavily dependent on a thorough understanding of the industry in which the companies are operating. The discrete growth model permits the critical link to be made between a company's growth opportunities and its value. There is no way that thorough fundamental research can be undertaken, whether in the spotlight or the shadows, without a commitment to industry and competitive analysis.

The implication is that there are important economies of re-search scope associated with concentration of individual research on one or possibly two industries. It is hardly surprising that profes-sional security research is organized in this manner. For our pur-poses, the key point is that the same principle applies to research in the shadows. The chances of identifying true discount stocks de-pend very much on the researcher's knowledge of competition within the industry. Given this knowledge, the problem of scarce data in the shadows can be partially circumvented by using the stock's market price in the discrete growth model to infer the firm's life cycle phase and future return, for qualitative comparison with the industry fundamentals.

For investors who wish to diversify across shadow stocks, the depth of fundamental research outlined above is very time-consum-ing. To avoid this cost, one has to concentrate on a few industries, as mentioned above, or employ the kind of statistical and technical research described in the next chapter, or use the screening pro-cedures discussed in Part III. The trade-off is that, for stocks which appear to be undervalued relative to the statistical or screening norm, there is no way of confirming whether they deserve it with-out recourse to the fundamental analysis of this chapter.

7

QUANTITATIVE INFORMATION ON THE DISCOUNT

This chapter describes how the fundamental valuation methods of Chapter 6 can be supplemented by statistical techniques based on price-earnings multiplier models. After introducing the latter, simple approaches to earnings projection are described, followed by a method for extrapolating earnings forecasts from the spotlight into the shadows.

STATISTICAL ANALYSIS IN THE SHADOWS

Statistical analysis has an ambiguous record of performance prediction in the investment world. Most commonly, statistical analysis is used with charting in the technical analysis of historical price and trading volume. But as Jack Francis, of the academic school expresses it: "The patterns described by technical analysts . . . can also be found in random numbers or in ink blots. . . . A reasonable person who objectively studied the existing literature would most likely conclude that technical analysis tools were (in some cases) crude attempts to measure risk or (in most cases) not worth performing at all."

Here the concern is not with the analysis of stock price data per se, but with a statistical form of fundamental analysis involving earnings extrapolation and valuation in a cross-sectional setting. In terms of performance, the statistical approach to earnings valuation at the very least describes how the market values securities in terms of common variables.

This chapter focuses on the best-known of the statistical valuation approaches, the price earnings multiplier model. The variables affecting corporate value are examined for a set of individual stocks to obtain an average statistical relationship between those variables and the price earnings ratio. The actual price performance of individual stocks is then compared with the performance suggested by the valuation relationship. Below average actual price performance indicates that the stock may be undervalued, and vice versa.

Unfortunately, the statistical relationships are not stable. These models, therefore, have to be used with great care. Small deviations between actual prices and those predicted by the models cannot be used to classify a stock as either under- or overvalued. On the other hand, large deviations can provide a strong signal for use as a supplement to fundamental research of the type described in Chapter 6. As one would expect, the chances of finding large deviations in the spotlight are questionable. In the shadows, by contrast, the chances of finding significant mispricing are very much greater. Hence, the special utility of shadow statistical analysis.

PRICE-EARNINGS MULTIPLIER MODEL

The model is designed to compare a particular stock's price-earnings ratio (P/E) with its statistically normal P/E ratio. The notion of a statistical P/E was first suggested by Whitbeck and Kisor. As a theory behind the P/E, they chose a special case of the discrete growth model, namely, the constant growth formula. By using that formula, the P/E can be expressed as a function of the dividend payout ratio, the anticipated dividend growth rate, and a risk measure which determines the cost of equity.

Using a sample of 135 stocks within the S&P 500, during the period 1960–1961, Whitbeck and Kisor estimated a constant growth model designed to explain the differences in P/Es across companies. In their analysis, they corrected for a major problem inherent in all P/E valuation analysis: A company's earnings are directly correlated with the GNP of the economy, and, like GNP, tend to fluctuate cyclically over time. To compensate, they obtained normalized earnings figures from analysts which represent forecasts of earnings during the middle of a business cycle. By dividing the current market price by normalized earnings they computed a normalized P/E ratio. Within this framework, the relationship shown in Table 7.1 was found.

TABLE 7.1   Whitbeck-Kisor Statistical P/E Model

P/E	= 8.2 + 1.5 (growth rate) + 6.7 (payout ratio) − 0.2 (risk)
where P/E	= current price divided by normalized earnings
growth rate	= projected percentage growth rate in normal earnings.
payout ratio	= ratio of dividends paid to earnings
risk	= percentage standard deviation around the projected growth rate of normalized earnings.

Source: Volkert Whitbeck and Manown Kisor, "A New Tool in Investment Decision Making," *Financial Analysts Journal*, (May/June 1963). Reprinted with permission.

As opposed to most models employed by contrarians, this model does not select stocks with a low P/E in an absolute sense, but rather stocks with an actual P/E below what the statistical valuation suggests it should be. In other words, the model selects stocks with low P/Es relative to the level suggested by the company's growth, risk, and dividend payout.

The model was tested for its ability to identify stocks as over- or undervalued. The results are shown in Table 7.2. The portfolio of stocks identified as undervalued by the model outperformed the S&P 500 in each of the four years studied by a substantial margin of more than eight percent per year. Moreover, stocks identified as overvalued underperformed the market by an equally wide margin.

Unfortunately, these results are not conclusive. As William Sharpe, the father of the beta risk coefficient and the capital asset pricing model, points out, the returns in Table 7.2 are not adjusted for risk. Furthermore, the risk measure employed by Whitbeck and Kisor may have been "a poor surrogate for market sensitivity," because it did not discriminate between systematic and diversifiable risk. In addition, since Whitbeck and Kisor did not include measures of statistical significance, the findings may in part be no more than a matter of luck.

With these limitations in mind, the study was repeated about five years later by Malkiel and Cragg. They used estimates made by investment firms for 175 stocks from amongst the largest companies in the S&P 500 over the period 1961 to 1965. The valuation equations obtained for each of the years are shown in the following table.

Measurements of systematic risk and growth estimates obtained from a wider sample of analysts gave Malkiel and Cragg somewhat different results than those of Whitbeck and Kisor. Comparison of the equations in Tables 7.1 and 7.3 for the year 1961 demonstrates that growth and risk take on added importance in the Malkiel and Cragg study while the explanatory role of the payout ratio diminishes. In addition, the 1970 study found that a great deal (up to 75 percent in 1963) of the variation in P/E ratios across companies is explained by these three variables. Malkiel and Cragg also tested the robustness of their model. They found that the substitution of historical data for growth, dividend payout, and risk reduced the explanatory power of the model substantially. However, when the expected standard deviation in earnings was used instead

TABLE 7.2 Valuation Performance of the Statistical P/E Model

	Undervalued Group		S&P 500		Overvalued Group	
	3 Month's Change	Cumulative Change	3 Month's Change	Cumulative Change	3 Month's Change	Cumulative Change
9/23/60 Study	+11.9%	+11.9%	+ 6.6%	+ 6.6%	+5.7%	+ 5.7%
12/23/60 Study	+16.8	+30.7	+12.3	+19.7	+8.3	+14.5
3/24/61 Study	+ 3.0	+34.6	+ 1.0	+20.9	−1.4	+12.9
6/23/61 Study	+ 3.2	+38.9	+ 2.4	+23.8	+2.1	+15.3

Source: Volkert Whitbeck and Manown Kisor, "A New Tool in Investment Decision Making," *Financial Analysts Journal*, May/June 1963. Reprinted with permission.

TABLE 7.3   Statistical Valuation Equations

1961: P/E =	4.73 + 3.28 (growth)	+ 2.05 (payout)	− .83 (risk)
1962:	11.06 + 1.75	+ .78	− 1.61
1963:	2.94 + 2.55	+ 7.62	− .27
1964:	6.71 + 2.05	+ 5.33	− .89
1965:	.96 + 2.74	+ 5.01	− .35

Source: Burton Malkiel and John Cragg, "Expectations and the Structure of Share Prices," *American Economic Review,* September 1970. Reprinted with permission.

of the historic beta as a risk factor, the results of the model were basically the same.

On the other hand, it is evident from Table 7.3 that the statistical valuation expression is highly unstable. In 1961, for example, growth was the most important variable, to judge by its coefficient of 3.28. In 1962, risk became a much more important factor, while in 1963, the payout ratio increased in importance.

Why all this instability? Part of the problem is the model's assumption of a linear relationship between the P/E ratio and the valuation variables. By contrast, looking back at the discrete growth model in Table 6.1, we see that the relationships hardly seem linear. Moreover, the present value factor associated with the time profile of future growth is missing from the statistical analysis. The statistical estimates try to offset this specification error by overloading the coefficients to compensate for what is missing. However, the expected present value factors are continually changing, so the valuation expression is correspondingly unstable.

Working with investment firm predictions, Malkiel and Cragg were unable to duplicate the predictive ability of Whitbeck and Kisor's model. In two of the five years the model accounted for some of the variation in actual returns; in two years the predictions amounted to nothing, and in one year the model gave the wrong result in that the so-called overvalued stocks did better than the undervalued stocks. The investment firm expectations apparently contained no information that was not already reflected in the stock prices. But all of this was done primarily in the informational spotlight, where investors cannot expect to earn superior returns easily.

SHADOW APPLICATION OF P/E MODEL

In the shadows, there is every reason to believe that things might be different. Carvell, Pari, and Sullivan have repeated the study for the period 1980 to 1984, using the analysts' expectations reported on the I/B/E/S tape for a sample of 600 stocks in the spotlight and on the periphery of the shadows. The growth factor was based on the two-year implied growth rate in earnings calculated by using the analysts' earnings estimates for the next two years. The standard deviation in the one-year earnings forecasts was employed as the risk proxy.

To get a sense for how the model might work in the shadows, they took account of the fact that the model is unable to discriminate sharply between correctly and incorrectly valued stocks. Rather than analyzing the performance of all stocks determined to be undervalued by the model, they included only the 30 most undervalued stocks in the test portfolio. As expected, this set of extremely undervalued securities comprised mainly stocks in the shadows and on the periphery. The performance of the sample relative to the market portfolio is shown in Table 7.4.

During each of the four years (1980 to 1984) included in the study, the portfolio of undervalued stocks outperformed the market as a whole. Over the four years, the returns on the undervalued portfolio exceeded 37 percent on average, compared to the market's 19 percent. Moreover, the undervalued portfolio was not found to

TABLE 7.4   Performance of Statistically Undervalued (Neglected) Stocks

Time Period	Annual Market Returns	Undervalued Portfolio Returns	Undervalued Portfolio Beta
1980–1981	34.4%	69.8%	1.078
1981–1982	−9.1	−8.1	.626
1982–1983	49.1	72.3	1.031
1983–1984	1.6	14.6	.853

Source: S. Carvell, R. Pari, and T. Sullivan, "The Determinants of Price Earnings Ratios: An Expectations Approach." Working Paper 1986, Bentley College, Waltham, MA.

be much riskier than the market. The higher returns exhibited by the undervalued stocks, in other words, were not due to higher systematic risk.

Unfortunately, there are two problems with the use of an expectational model for neglected stock valuation. First, like all statistical valuation models, the coefficients are not very stable. Second, the values for expected growth and risk are not available for neglected stocks in the deep shadows, which, by definition, are not covered by research analysts contributing to the I/B/E/S system.

To get around the first problem, all variables including the valuation relationship itself could be re-estimated continually, in order to ensure that the valuation expression captures the most recent expectations about the time profile of future growth and anything else that may be missing in the linear model. I/B/E/S publishes estimates of this type in its "Monthly Comments." Each month's Comments contains a reestimated model. For illustration we have included a sample from the March 1986 "I/B/E/S Monthly Comments."

I/B/E/S updates the model's parameters each month so that any shifts in the market's perception of the importance of growth, risk, and payout in determining P/E ratios will be picked up. In addition, the estimated model from the previous twelve months is displayed, so that investors can get a feel for the changes that the model, as a whole, has undergone during that time.

For instance, one can see that the coefficient for growth in the model has gone from .6 to .94 in less than six months. That difference may not seem very large, but the shift represents more than a 50 percent increase in the weight associated with growth as a determinant of a company's theoretical P/E ratio. The coefficient for risk is even more unstable. It moves from $-.01$ to $-.03$ to .04 then to .02 in a little over six months. The implausible positive coefficients, suggesting that risk has a favorable impact on the P/E ratio, plus the low percentage of variation in P/E ratios explained during late 1985 and early 1986, show that the model had difficulty capturing the market's pricing process at that time. Owing to this problem, I/B/E/S is continuing research to improve the model. Alternatively, the investor or manager may want to estimate a specific model for market segments or industries of special interest, particularly those in the shadows.

TABLE 7.5   I/B/E/S Statistical Valuation Model

	P/E =	(growth)	(risk)	(payout)	% of P/E Explained
Feb 1986	0.94	+0.02	+0.08	−0.86	31%
Jan 1986	0.87	+0.02	+0.07	+0.15	35
Dec 1985	0.83	+0.00	+0.06	+1.31	33
Nov 1985	0.82	+0.04	+0.10	−1.55	34
Oct 1985	0.60	−0.03	+0.06	+2.86	40
Sep 1985	0.61	−0.00	+0.06	+1.84	28
Aug 1985	0.61	−0.01	+0.04	+1.84	42
Jul 1985	0.69	−0.01	+0.04	+2.38	46
Jun 1985	0.59	−0.01	+0.04	+2.93	40
May 1985	0.70	+0.01	+0.05	+0.47	48
Apr 1985	0.67	−0.01	+0.06	+0.75	49
Mar 1985	0.58	−0.02	+0.06	+1.80	48

Source: I/B/E/S Monthly Comments 1985–1986, The Institutional Broker's Estimate System," published by Lynch, Jones and Ryan, N.Y.C. Reprinted with permission.

The second challenge, more critical for successful investment, is to obtain better estimates than the market consensus for each company's growth, risk, and payout ratio. The lack of expectational data in the deep shadows provides a special challenge and opportunity in this regard. A brief review is presented below of some simple methods for projecting a company's future earnings growth and the risk surrounding that growth rate in the shadows.

EARNINGS ESTIMATES

Basically there are three ways of getting at earnings forecasts. The first is to use fundamental research in an attempt to project the financial statements into the future. This is a time-consuming task in the shadows—even with the indirect methods suggested in Chapter 6. The second approach involves using the market's information network. The latter is composed of other analysts and clearinghouses for earnings estimates. Of course, by definition, there are few if any analysts covering stocks in the shadows. Therefore, this approach is most useful on the periphery, where one, two, or three analysts may provide useful investment advice. In addition, internal information may be obtained from sources within the company itself. Precisely because shadow stocks are apparently less accessible in the sense that they might not have investor relations officers, any contact that can be established with them is likely to be especially rewarding.

The third approach, of particular use in the deep shadows where no analysts' forecasts are available, is graphically based. Using a time series of past earnings, investors can plot the path of a company's earnings. The time series trend can be established either visually or statistically, each method having its own advantages. With the course of past earnings plotted, the investor must then determine whether, and by how much, the company is likely to deviate from the historical path in the near and intermediate future.

To illustrate the steps and complications involved, the annual earnings stream for NCR is graphed in Figure 7.1. NCR was selected for illustration because, as a well-known stock, the earnings estimate from the graphical procedures could be compared with forecast data from other sources, thus illustrating the hazards of this

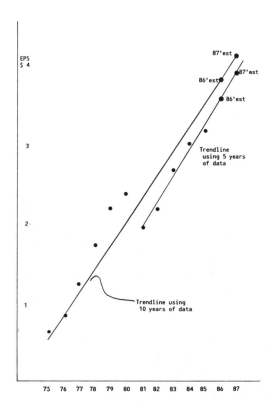

Figure 7.1   Scatter plot and earnings trendline for NCR 1975–1985.

approach even in the spotlight. Annual rather than quarterly data was employed to avoid the complications of seasonality.

Once the line has been drawn to the "analyst's visual satisfaction," the most direct procedure would be to simply extend it to obtain an extrapolation estimate of the next few years' earnings. In the case of this graph the estimates for NCR would be $3.80 for 1986 and $4.10 for 1985. Given NCR's 1985 EPS of $3.15, this corresponds to annual growth rates of 20.6 percent and 7.9 percent, respectively, or a two average rate of 14.3 percent. Needless to say, similar results could be obtained from a statistical regression analysis. Some might argue that statistical projections would be more accurate. But all projections based on historical data embody a fundamental dilemma that is particularly acute in the shadows.

On the one hand, there is the need for sufficient data to develop a statistically significant relationship. On the other, there is the need for currently relevant data. This latter requirement is often difficult to satisfy. Industries, as we saw in Chapter 6, go through very different phases of development. Companies change whole product lines and add new divisions sometimes doing business in a completely different industry. Over time, the essence of the company shifts. In the case of NCR, for example, between 1980 and 1981, there was a strong downturn in earnings from $2.30 per share to $1.93. NCR was not alone; Sperry, Data General, and IBM, among others, all experienced an earnings decline during this period caused by the emergence of the microcomputer. Taking this industry transition into account, one might argue that earnings projections should be based only on the data from 1981 onwards. But extrapolation of the five-year trend line for NCR results in 1986 and 1987 EPS forecasts of only $3.57 and $3.90, respectively, with a corresponding average two-year growth rate of 11.3 percent.

This kind of earnings instability cannot be easily dealt with by using more sophisticated statistical analysis. All forecasting methods assume some form of stability in the structure of the historical data. It may be complex substructure revealed by decomposition of the data, as in the Box Jenkins method, for example. Whatever the case, the method depends on the stability of the historical structure to forecast the future. No forecasting method can predict through and beyond a discontinuity in the structure of the time series data.

The statistical valuation equation discussed earlier has the advantage of being estimated within a single period using data across a sample of stocks, and hence assumes only that the coefficients will remain constant over two periods between the times of estimation and valuation. Time series earnings forecasting requires a stable data structure over all the periods needed to get a statistically significant equation, in addition to the forecasting period.

Unfortunately, earnings instability is particularly acute in the shadows. First, there is the random company-specific risk that tends to be greater for the smaller firms found in the shadows and obscures the underlying trend in earnings. Second, there is the additional jump risk to which shadow investors are exposed. The only advantage of looking at shadow earnings rather than directly at price data is that earnings are not further distorted by the long periods between shadow information events.

Nevertheless, it is not only dangerous but also rarely a benefit to rely on historical earnings patterns in the shadows. If the trend line happens to be stable, the chances are it is already reflected in the price. And if it is stable and is not reflected in the price, there is probably little of interest happening to the firm and it may stay neglected.

How then, can one get at future earnings estimates in the shadows? Visual examination of the earnings data may help to identify breaks in the data, but it cannot assist in deciding whether the trend after the most recent break will continue. Like all forecasting problems, the trick is to find some form of relatively stable relationship which can be projected into the future. There is indirect evidence in the return data used to test the beta risk model that the relative volatility of a company's earnings compared to the market, or its industry, is more stable than the pattern of the company's earnings over time. The next section describes an earnings estimation approach for the shadows which is built on the presumed stability of the volatility rather then level, of a neglected firm's earnings relative to its industry.

EXTRAPOLATING FROM THE SPOTLIGHT

To obtain an earnings forecast for a completely neglected stock, the analysts' forecasts for companies in the industry spotlight can be projected into the shadows. For the sake of illustration, consider the information provided by I/B/E/S in their Monthly Summary Data Service. In that service, composite EPS forecasts are made for all major industrial groups. This is accomplished by averaging the consensus EPS estimates weighted by the number of shares for all companies that are followed by analysts. Industry EPS forecasts are provided for each of the next two years. Comparison with the current industry EPS immediately yields the corresponding growth rate forecasts.

In order to project the industry forecasts on to a neglected stock in the deep shadows, one needs the stock's earnings volatility relative to the industry; that is, a form of "EPS beta." Instead of estimating the responsiveness of the stock's returns to market portfolio returns, the volatility of a company's EPS growth is needed relative to its industry's EPS growth. Finding the EPS beta is a matter of plotting, or statistically regressing, company EPS growth against industry EPS growth. In the case of I/B/E/S, updated annual data is reported, so some ten years of annual data is usually required to get an estimate of the EPS beta, or the slope of the graph of company EPS growth against industry EPS growth.

Even in the case of these EPS betas, it is not always easy to get estimates that are both reliable (based on sufficient data) and current (based only on relevant data). With annual data, one is forced to go quite far back in time to get an estimate. Quarterly or monthly data, which is virtually impossible to get in the shadows, would be preferable. In many cases, EPS betas can be obtained only by employing a good dose of visual judgment. For firms with short listing periods, the exercise may indeed become futile.

If an EPS beta can be obtained, the next step is to multiply it by the estimated change in the industry EPS growth for the year. To return to the example of NCR, ten years of annual EPS growth data from I/B/E/S, for 1975 to 1985, on the company and the computer manufacturing industry, yields an EPS beta of 1.7. The projected EPS growth rates for the computer manufacturing industry for 1986 and 1987 were 0.6 percent and 31 percent. (These growth forecasts reflect the sharp temporary downturn that was expected in the industry). Multiplying by NCR's EPS beta of 1.7 produces annual industry-related growth rates for the company of 1.0 percent in 1986 and 52.7 in 1987, or an average two-year growth rate of 26.9 percent. The latter is well above the five-year company trend line estimate, derived in the previous section, of 11.3 percent.

Which of these two growth rate forecasts should be used in the statistical valuation model to get NCR's theoretical P/E? The company's historical growth rate is not the same as the industry-related growth. On the other hand, the company's historical growth trend cannot simply be projected into the future. There are clear limits to what can be done with statistical security research. Qualitative, nonstatistical, fundamental research is needed at this point to get a better sense for NCR's future growth potential. In the absence of such research, one simple but arbitrary approach would be to simply average the historical company and industry related trends. For NCR, this yields an EPS growth forecast of 19 percent.

Still needed as inputs to the valuation model are risk and dividend payout estimates. In the I/B/E/S valuation model, risk is expressed in terms of the coefficient of variation in the long-run growth rate. Multiplying NCR's EPS beta of 1.7 by the coefficient of variation in analysts' long-run growth forecasts for the computer manufacturing industry of 14 percent, one obtains a risk estimate for NCR of 24 percent. With respect to the dividend payout ratio, it is reasonable to assume that average historical values can be employed without adjustment, because dividends tend to be relatively stable in the short run. If it is assumed that the historical NCR payment of 25 percent is stable, the same can be used as the future dividend estimate. Substituting the growth, risk, and dividend estimates into the February 1986 I/B/E/S valuation model in Table 7.5 yields a theoretical P/E for NCR of 19.5. Compared to NCR's actual P/E of 11.6 in January 1986, this particular statistical analysis would suggest that NCR was undervalued.

On the other hand, if the company growth trend of 11.3 percent had been used in the valuation equation, rather than an average between the company and industry growth rates, the theoretical P/E would have been 12.6. On the basis of the latter, NCR with an actual P/E of 11.6 would not have been regarded as undervalued. Apparently, the market was valuing the company on the basis of its historical EPS growth (11.3 percent) over the last five years. NCR was not viewed as benefiting from the greater growth forecast (26.9 percent) associated with the computer industry as a whole.

LINK BETWEEN STATISTICAL
AND FUNDAMENTAL RESEARCH

When the statistical research of this chapter is combined with the qualitative fundamental research of Chapter 6, it becomes clear that at a P/E of 11.6 NCR was correctly valued. The fundamental analysis of Chapter 6 showed that NCR was one of the firms stuck in the middle of the industry, with neither a clear-cut high-perceived-value strategy, nor a competitive low-delivered-cost approach. The company's strategy was obscure in 1980, and not much had changed in the intervening six years to 1986. The market was apparently fully aware of NCR's performance and valued the company appropriately, which might have been anticipated, since with an analyst following of 26, the stock was very much in the spotlight.

All of this demonstrates the danger of using statistical research on its own. NCR was a spotlight stock. Nevertheless, the statistics alone might have lead to a buy decision, based on the erroneous conclusion that the company was undervalued. The chances of being led astray are even greater in the shadows, where the statistics are perforce less reliable. Given its dubious record on both an aggregate and individual stock basis, statistical investment research should always be used as a complement to fundamental research in the shadows.

A good example of the combined use of both approaches is provided by the partially neglected stock of Commodore International. The fundamental analysis of Chapter 6 identified the company as a potentially undervalued stock at the end of 1980. The interesting question is whether this was confirmed by the statistical valuation method. Commodore's actual P/E at the time was approximately 13. But its recent history from 1978 to 1980 was dominated by phenomenal earnings growth; in 1980, analysts were forecasting additional growth of approximately 50 percent. All the statistical valuation models were placing a high value on growth at the time. For example, based on the Carvell, Pari, and Sullivan model, Commodore's 1980 statistical P/E was 21, compared to the actual P/E of 13. Despite the absence of dividends and relatively high risk, Commodore could be classified as undervalued according to the statistical model. Taken together with the fundamental analysis in Chapters 5 and 6, this definitely would have signalled the identification of a discount stock.

In general, the combined use of statistical and fundamental analysis requires a good measure of judgment for its successful implementation in the shadows. Owing to the lack of analysts' forecasts, the judgment component is much higher in the deep shadows than in the spotlight. The need for additional judgment in the shadows is precisely what creates not only the analytical difficulty, but also the opportunities for outperforming the market averages.

8

TRACKING THE INFORMATION SPOTLIGHT

The big payoff to investment in the shadows starts when a true discount stock begins to draw attention. What are the signs that a neglected discount stock will actually emerge from the shadows? Can one track the attention of analysts? This chapter discusses first, the factors that act as a catalyst in attracting analysts' attention to neglected stocks, and second, the indicators that can be used to monitor the flow of research popularity over time.

CATALYSTS OF THE POPULARITY FLOW

The flow of investment attention is critical to the superior performance of neglected stocks. As institutions and other market participants buy numerous large blocks of a stock, the price typically rises rapidly. It is this movement from the shadows towards the spotlight which produces the phenomenal returns that make the neglected sector of the market so attractive. Thus, even if numerous discount stocks have been identified in the shadows, the rest of the market must first recognize this fact before the really superior returns can be anticipated. Without this recognition, one is stuck with wall-flowers producing acceptable returns, but short of the explosive performance that would accompany their discovery by the investment community.

What is it that attracts institutions and others to a particular stock in the shadows? One might argue that if an investor or manager has discovered a high potential discount stock, the institutions will discover it too. If diligent analysis has selected a portfolio comprised of the financially strongest, most undervalued shadow stocks, the probability should be quite high that some of these will be discovered. But there are probably hundreds of bargains in the shadows at any time. What exactly are the catalysts of investment attention?

In answering this question, it is useful to recall Chapter 1, where it was pointed out that change is one of the key factors that attract analysts, because it enhances the value of information. There are two types of change or event which alter the valuation of a stock. One is natural or economic events, like new product innovations, or natural disasters, such as the Bhopal incident. The other is information events. Large block trading, insiders trading, and managerial reorganizations fall under this category. Valuation changes caused by these factors are often inferential.

Economic Events and the Popularity Flow

For any natural or economic event to affect a stock's price, it must also be accompanied by an information event. If a company discovers oil, and this is not known, then one would not expect the stock price to move. In general, however, information events tend to accompany economic events. Although companies will be more likely to disclose good information than bad, significant economic events of any type are difficult to cover up in an information-based society.

The first and most obvious example of an economic event likely to trigger a popularity flow towards a neglected stock is merger activity. Nothing attracts institutional investors like a merger proposal, a clear case of flies to honey. They earn high short-term profits, and are cleared out of their positions by the merging company. Of course, no one can tell which companies in the shadows are likely to be merger candidates. In general, it is those companies that are financially sound, fundamentally strong, and statistically undervalued that have the higher probability of being merger candidates.

A second category of economic event to watch for are product innovations and new patents, especially when accompanied by an information event which rates the likely success of the new product—for example, a product's acceptance by industry experts, followed by positive reports in the industry's professional journals. Product introductions may also attract attention; Apple's micro comes to mind. Other economic events include the first-time declaration of a dividend, or an increased dividend that is likely to be sustained into the foreseeable future.

Another powerful economic event likely to attract institutional interest is unexpectedly high earnings. Precisely because they were not anticipated, unexpected earnings attract attention. Known as SUEs, or standardized unexpected earnings, stocks that have exhibited high SUEs have proven to provide superior performance in numerous studies, notably those by Latane and Jones.

By comparing actual EPS to forecasted EPS one can identify those stocks that had the highest unexpected earnings. This is usually expressed as unexpected earnings per unit of risk, which controls for the range, or standard deviation of the expected EPS. SUEs are obtained by subtracting actual EPS from the expected EPS and dividing by the standard deviation of the forecasted EPS. In the shadows, forecasted EPS may be obtained by simple naive extrapolation of the historical EPS trendline as in Figure 7.1. Simple statistical extrapolation is the most common form of EPS forecasting that is likely to be used in the shadows and, therefore, provides a reasonable basis for estimating the expected EPS.

SUEs are best used as a comparative measure. Since earnings, on the whole, are a function of the economy, unexpectedly strong economic growth will cause many firms to exhibit high SUEs. To gauge how large a SUE is necessary to invoke institutional interest, one can again employ the I/B/E/S service. I/B/E/S publishes the 40 highest quarterly SUEs each month. If the SUE of a discount stock is near those values, then it is time to track institutional interest. Like all investors, institutions prefer positive surprises and will hope that the stock will continue to surprise the market positively in the future, bringing along with it the excess returns typically associated with positive SUEs.

Information Events and the Popularity Flow

Information events, as opposed to economic events, that are likely to spur institutional interest include insider's buying (disclosed by the SEC and available through, among others, Vickers On-Line), stock splits, managerial reorganizations, and the addition of well-known managers, Lee Iacocca of Chrysler and John Scully of Apple being highly visible examples. Some of these may, of course, have a subsequent economic impact, but it is the initial positive announcement that tends to trigger institutional interest. In general, articles that appear in popular or industry journals positively depicting the company's future are information events to watch for.

Just as each of the economic and information events discussed above is likely to attract institutional and other investors, there are events which will dissuade institutions from investing in a company's stock. Large negative earnings surprises, litigations, product recalls, a competitor's product innovation which may replace the company's main product, or a decrease in dividends are just a few examples of these. If a neglected firm has suffered from any of these events, then a reevaluation of its status as a discount stock is called for. If there is little price reaction to these events, the stock may be overvalued. Conversely, if the price drops precipitously, the stock may be undervalued. Such market overreaction constitutes a classic contrarian investment opportunity.

The timely identification of positive or negative events that catalyze attention requires a good measure of what might be called a "wide awake" approach. The investor or manager is surrounded by clues to possible shifts in analyst attention. What's needed is sufficient awareness to recognize the clues when they present themselves. In the final analysis, when it comes to information collection in the shadows, there is no substitute for an entrepreneurial approach, based on the identification of an unrecognized idea or a new trend.

MONITORING THE FIRST PHASE
OF THE POPULARITY FLOW

The attention of analysts and investors may be monitored with the same criteria used to identify neglected stocks. When one is studying the popularity of stocks moving from the shadows into the spotlight, attention must be concentrated on readily available variables, sensitive to timely shifts in the relative neglect of a stock. With this in mind, the criteria employed to identify neglected stocks can be reviewed to assess their suitability as a monitoring device. The criteria discussed in Chapter 4 were the following: listing period, number of shareholders, relative volume and block trading, institutional holdings, and analysts' coverage.

The first shadow criterion mentioned above is not a very good measure of a stock's neglect in a dynamic framework. The listing period will not change that much over the short run, regardless of how much attention is afforded the company in question. It is, therefore, of little use as a monitoring device of the popularity flow towards shadow stocks.

The next criterion suffers from a similar problem. Although the number of shareholders can change over the longer run, this variable does not move much over the period of a year. The lack of sensitivity to the information spotlight lessens its usefulness as possible measure of the popularity flow. Furthermore, the number of shareholders is not readily available for many stocks. When available, the figure is typically updated only once a year. The lack of timely updates further decreases its usefulness in monitoring the popularity flow.

The last three variables, namely, relative volume and large block trading, institutional holdings, and analysts' coverage, together provide the means for monitoring the popularity flow. The most important concept to keep in mind is the loose demarcation of the shadows. Exactly where the shadows brighten into the spotlight is not easily determined.

An idealized version of the popularity flow is depicted in Figure 8.1. It is based on the 80/20 rule, or the principle of declining returns to information and popularity. The flow of popularity begins with a neglected stock that has no institutional holders, no analysts' coverage, very low relative volume, and very few large block trades. The first signs of the popularity flow begin with a rise in the stock's average daily relative volume and/or an increase in the average large block trades taking place for the day. The increase in the volume and size of the trades for the stock are the footprints of increasing institutional interest.

However, increasing volume may mean nothing, unless accompanied by upward price movement. Increasing volume by itself may simply be due to the liquidity needs of the current shareholders. Rising prices are the first tip-off that buying pressure has begun

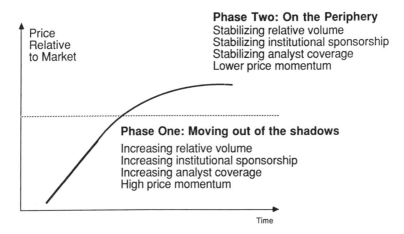

Figure 8.1   Idealized popularity flow.

by those who think the company is selling at a discount. The forces that move prices are associated with shifts in the average shareholder's valuation of the company. During the process of increasing popularity, upward price momentum must be observed.

Institutional Discovery and Analyst Coverage

Institutional discovery and purchases of neglected discount stocks are the catalyst necessary for a successful transition from the shadows to the spotlight. Institutional holdings are of primary interest, because institutions tend to create excess demand beyond the available supply of shares and willingness of others to go short. The excess demand caused by increased institutional buying activity causes the neglected stock's price to rise in response to the excess demand pressure.

Analyst coverage is an important part of the popularity flow for several reasons. First, major institutions will typically limit any holdings in stocks that are not covered by professional analysts. Any serious position by an institution in a stock will probably be accompanied by some analyst coverage. The second reason is that analysts often instigate a stampede amongst the institutional herd. One institution may take a chance investing in a stock that is not followed by security analysts. But institutions have a tendency to herd together, investing only where other institutions have already cleared a safe path. The first few institutional investors are therefore not easily attracted. However, once one or two have shown the way, others tend to follow, although not in as many numbers and in smaller positions, if there is no analyst covering the stock on an ongoing basis.

Moreover, analysts provide some assurance that no major negative news is imminent. The last thing that an institutional investor wants is to observe the drop in price of a newly acquired issue because of some information that should have been uncovered earlier. Institutions are by their very nature highly risk-averse. Having an analyst or two watching their investments provides both a measure of safety and a possible scapegoat if something unexpected happens.

This is especially important in the shadows, because most neglected stocks are relatively thinly traded, and their prices are quite volatile in response to any information. Both positive and negative information may cause sizable price fluctuations in shadow stocks. In particular, owing to the relatively high levels of informational uncertainty, stocks in the shadows are especially sensitive to bad information. Current analyst coverage provides the extra confidence that institutional investors require to take substantial long positions in neglected stocks.

Once the footprints of the institutional traders have been detected, the investor must constantly monitor the stock. This monitoring process should include close scrutiny of the stock's professional analyst coverage and its institutional holdings, measured by numbers of institutions and the total number of shares held by institutions. As discussed in Chapter 4, both institutional ownership and analyst coverage are available from numerous information data bases.

Close monitoring is necessary because institutional buying pressure can take up to three months or more before it is publicly reported (see Chapter 4 for periodicity of neglect measures). Therefore, printed listings of institutional investment patterns, like the Standard and Poor's Stock Guide, are less useful for monitoring the popularity flow than they are for identifying stocks which currently occupy the shadows. Use of computerized services like Vickers On-Line are particularly useful in monitoring the institutional popularity flow for stocks in the shadows because of the timeliness of the updates.

The timeliness of the updates in analyst coverage increases its appropriateness as a measure of the popularity flow. This is highlighted by the contrast with the long time lag in institutional holding reports. An increase in analyst coverage will be picked up within a month. The on-line service provided by I/B/E/S, known as I/B/O/L, and the ICARUS Service available on the Dow Jones News/Retrieval service provide analyst attention data on a regular basis.

THE SECOND PHASE OF THE POPULARITY FLOW

Once the popularity flow has taken off, will it continue, bringing even more price appreciation with it? If the process is to continue, the analysts who now cover the stock must give favorable reports on the company. If it is assumed that the investor's research is correct, the analysts are likely to identify the stock as a highly undervalued investment opportunity. This will spur more institutional buying pressure, maintaining the stock's upward price momentum.

With more institutional buying interest, more analysts are attracted to the company, casting more light on the company's true value and eliminating the last hint of the shadow. Upon entering this phase of the popularity flow, there can be numerous successions of increased institutional interest, spurring increased analyst coverage, inducing more institutional buying, and so on. However, the price momentum probably will not be as great as in the early phase of the popularity flow. The 80/20 rule begins to affect the value of additional information, with the stock no longer being as undervalued as it was at the start of the institutional discovery process. Eventually the upward price momentum will cease when the stock's value has reached its ceiling as determined by all interested investors.

Thus, the popularity flow can be broken down into two broad phases. The first phase is characterized by the initial volume increases and price rises. Phase one occurs for almost all stocks in the shadows as they begin to move into the domain of institutional activity. However, once a stock is bought by the first wave of institutions, the nature of the popularity flow tends to change as it enters a second phase.

The chances of a successful second phase depend on the accuracy of the valuation process originally used to analyze the neglected stock. If the stock in question was heavily undervalued, then the second phase will almost assuredly occur, accompanied by upward price movement. If the stock was only moderately undervalued before the first phase, then the price increases that follow probably wipe out the original discount.

In general, price increases during the second phase of the popularity flow are much more uncertain than during the first phase. The stock price may decline if the stock becomes overvalued during the euphoria that often accompanies the first phase. Often professional analysis brings this fact to the attention of the investment community. A sour analyst's forecast at this point could wipe out much of the price appreciation experienced during the first phase.

In effect, the second phase of the popularity flow constitutes a period of consolidation in terms of relative volume, institutional holdings, and analysts' coverage. Whether or not the price continues to appreciate depends on whether the stock continues to be perceived as undervalued. The latter is often not clear-cut and is difficult to assess—Hence the increased price uncertainty associated with the final stages of the movement into the spotlight.

THE AMBIGUITY OF TECHNICAL ANALYSIS

Looking at the popularity flow as a two-phase process suggests the possibility of making more of technical analysis in the shadows than in the spotlight. Yet investment decisions based on past price and volume data have, at best, a dubious record. In the intense competition of the spotlight, prices reflect all available information almost instantaneously. In particular, prices embody any information that may be contained in historical price and volume data. Is it not possible, however, that with the lack of competition in the shadows, trends in price, volume, and analysts' attention can be exploited more profitably?

To explore this possibility, it is instructive to examine the popularity flow for stocks that have made the transition out of the shadows, to see whether any investment guidelines suggest themselves. The most interesting experience is provided by stocks with the most dramatic transitions, that is, by stocks with the highest returns, or price changes over an investment period. Table 8.1 lists some popularity flow data for seven representative companies from the 1984 list of largest percentage gainers in *Barron's*.

It should come as no surprise that most lists of winners are dominated by neglected stocks. The winners in Table 8.1 are no exceptions to that rule. If relatively neglected stocks are defined as those with three or fewer analysts covering them and less than 10 institutions owning shares, almost all of the eight stocks listed qualify as neglected stocks. With the exception of Hasbro-Bradley, which was on the fringes at the end of 1983, all of the other stocks were in the shadows.

To determine the relationship between the 1984 popularity flow and the phenomenal performance of these stocks over the year, one can analyze the increase in analysts' coverage and institutional ownership during the period.

TABLE 8.1 Popularity Flow and Performance

Name	Number of Analysts[1]			Number of Institutions[2]			Total Annual[3] Return	
	Dec. 1983	Dec. 1984	Dec. 1985	Dec. 1983	Dec. 1984	Dec. 1985	1984	1985
ICH Corp (A)* Size: $583 million	0	1	3	1	1	24	166.37%	42.84%
Mylan Labs (O) $302 million	0	2	5	5	12	34	185.85	45.54
Hasbro-Bradley (A) $573 million	3	5	9	11	36	130	125.93	42.11
Tootsie Roll (N) $87 million	1	1	2	6	16	20	86.42	84.00
Bic Corp (A) $140 million	2	2	1	6	9	17	88.78	118.37
Chicago-Milwaukee (N) $458 million	1	1	0	6	11	11	92.65	(27.22)
Price Comm (O) $48 million	0	0	1	5	12	22	186.06	(20.16)

*(A)–AMEX; (N)–NYSE; (O)–OTC

Source: [3]Barrons (December 1984); [2]S&P Stock Guide (1983–1985); [1]I/B/E/S (1983–1985).

Classic Movement Out of the Shadows

For the purposes of discussion, the companies in Table 8.1 can be separated into three groups. The first group, consisting of the first three companies in the table, provides classic examples of the movement from the shadows into the spotlight according to the 80/20 rule. Taking the first company, in December 1983, ICH had no analysts covering it and only one institutional sponsor. By December 1984 there was one security analyst covering the company, and the popularity flow had begun. During 1984, ICH experienced an increase in both average relative daily volume and large block trades. Although there was still only one institution showing on the books, there was no doubt that some additional institutional buying interest was associated with the stock's 166 percent price appreciation during the year. Phase one of the popularity flow was apparent during 1984.

However, for ICH the ride was not over. Due to a favorable forecast of future earnings, the popularity flow towards ICH continued. By December of 1985, ICH had three analysts covering it and 24 institutional owners. The stock's performance during 1985 was equally impressive, nearing 43 percent. Although the total return for the year was not as outstanding as the year before, 43 percent is nothing to complain about. For ICH the second phase of the popularity flow was highly profitable.

The second company, Mylan Labs, is another textbook example of price appreciation during both phase one and phase two of the popularity flow. In December 1983, Mylan had no analysts' coverage and only five institutions owning shares. By December 1984, there were two analysts and twelve institutions owning shares. Mylan's stock rose by more than 185 percent during that year. The popularity flow and its associated superior return performance were apparently at work again.

As before, Mylan's assent from the shadows was not yet over. With only two analysts covering its stock and twelve institutions owning shares, Mylan was on the fringes of the shadows. During 1985, the spotlight grew in intensity. By December, Mylan was regularly covered by five analysts and an impressive 34 institutional shareholders. This continuing popularity flow was accompanied by an impressive 45 percent share price appreciation.

The third company in the group, Hasbro-Bradley, provides an

interesting contrast, because it was already on the periphery of the shadows at the beginning of 1984. During 1984, it exhibited price appreciation of 126 percent, and by the end of 1984 H-B had five analysts covering it and 36 institutional investors. However, its popularity flow continued at an explosive rate. By the end of 1985, H-B had nine analysts providing forecasts and an impressive 130 institutions owning shares.

Although Hasbro-Bradley had explosive growth in institutional ownership and analyst coverage over 1985, its return was not much more than ICH's or Mylan's. As explained earlier, there are declining returns to increasing information. Like the other two companies, H-B was no longer neglected after the first stage of the popularity flow. In accordance with the 80/20 rule, once a stock is no longer in the shadows, further attention does not make as much difference.

The three stocks just analyzed have some interesting commonalities. All three experienced uninterrupted first and second phase popularity flows. From 1983 to 1984 and again from 1984 to 1985 all three companies exhibited increases in their analyst and/or institutional coverage. In addition, all three companies remained on the fringes of the shadows after the first phase of price growth. Moreover, there was no dramatic new information on these companies during the first two phases of the popularity flow. The common characteristics among these stocks, then, are as follows: all were neglected companies when the popularity flow began; each was still relatively neglected after the first year of the popularity flow; no substantial news was published during the first and second phases of the popularity flow.

Impact of Positive Information

Once a company has moved from the shadows into the spotlight of the big market players, significant changes in its true value are required for the price appreciation associated with the popularity flow to be maintained. Unless the company remains in the shadows after the first phase of the popularity flow, second-phase price appreciation may not be as dramatic. The underlying logic here is that increasing popularity increases the available information, thereby lowering the discount on a neglected stock. Once a company is popular, it takes either a much greater increase in information or a change in underlying value to maintain price momentum.

Tootsie Roll Ind., the first company in the second group of Table 8.1 illustrates the impact of significant new information on the popularity flow. Starting with one analyst and six institutions in December 1983, Tootsie Roll's institutional sponsorship grew to 16 by December 1984. Although there was no rise in the number of analysts covering the stock during the year, the stock's price did rise substantially, posting an 86 percent gain during the period. Phase one, although not quite like the ones followed by ICH and Mylan, was over. During 1985, however, Tootsie Roll was in the news. As a result, by December 1985, Tootsie Roll had two analysts and 20 institutional owners, and had posted another year of impressive price appreciation, topping 84 percent.

BIC Corp. also illustrates the impact of a changing intrinsic value. Although the stock experienced a drop in the number of analysts covering it during the second year of the popularity flow, it posted a second year of phenomenal price appreciation that was accompanied by a continued rise in institutional buying pressure. BIC was the continued rumored target of a merger during that period. This explains the second-year price appreciation and continued increase in institutional ownership. As a result, its reduced analyst coverage did not adversely affect its stock price.

Impact of Negative Information

Whereas the second group of companies in Table 8.1 illustrates the impact of significant positive information during the popularity flow, the third group shows the impact of negative information events. These stocks did not fare well during the second phase of the popularity flow. Chicago-Milwaukee had an impressive first phase with a price appreciation of almost 93 percent following an increase in popularity from six to 11 institutions. At that point C-M still fulfilled the criteria of being on the fringes of the shadows.

However, Chicago-Milwaukee did not fare well during the second phase of its popularity flow. The one analyst who followed the company apparently decided that the company no longer warranted attention. By dropping C-M from his or her coverage, the analyst, in effect, left the 11 institutions in the dark. Without any analysts' coverage, C-M was no longer attractive to new institutional investors. Its price dropped, possibly due to a change in true value, but also as a natural outgrowth of the higher informational uncertainty which surrounded the company after the decline in analysts' attention.

Owing to the impact of the 80/20 rule on the value of information, the loss of a single analyst means more than the loss of one analyst among several. The loss of one analyst did not adversely affect BIC, because it still had an analyst left covering it. By contrast, the loss of the single analyst covering C-M was a strong negative signal, since it eliminated the single source of professional public information on the company. The lesson here is that, apart from changes in underlying value, a company with only one analyst after the first stage of the popularity flow will suffer if the analyst decides not to cover the stock in the future.

In the final analysis, of course, what drives stock prices is the underlying value of the company. The popularity flow provides a bullish signal when it reflects the discovery of a neglected discount stock. But when the value of the stock shifts, the popularity flow by itself can be misleading. The data on the last company in Table 8.1 is a good case in point. Price Communication was on the fringe of the shadows after the first stage of the popularity flow with 12 institutions and no analysts' coverage. Thereafter, one analyst began to cover Price and the institutional ownership continued to increase. This normally would have indicated a high probability of a bullish second-stage popularity flow. But when the single analyst decided that the company was probably already overvalued, the stock price, needless to say, declined.

The variety of popularity flow and pricing patterns implicit in Table 8.1 illustrates how misleading it can be, even in the shadows, to base investment decisions on technical analysis alone. There is no overall consistency in the pattern of stocks that have made the transition into the spotlight; there is no way of predicting the timing and content of new information that may arrive during the popularity flow. No obvious investment rules are buried in Table 8.1.

On the other hand, when combined with fundamental and statistical analysis in the shadows, technical analysis of the popularity flow can provide the signal of impending recognition for previously neglected discount stocks. The high returns associated with the transition of discount stocks into the spotlight make this signal especially valuable, albeit difficult to interpret reliably.

THE VIRTUE OF PATIENCE IN THE SHADOWS

The most consistent way of capitalizing on the market discovery of discount stocks in the shadows is to buy and hold until the popularity flow materializes. Having made a commitment in the shadows, investors and managers must exhibit the patience and confidence necessary to allow the forces behind the information spotlight to work. If the security research has been properly done, the investor will be holding neglected stocks selling at a true discount. The best way to profit from that discount is to wait until major market participants, that is, the institutions, fall upon the stock and agree that it is undervalued. When word gets around that one institutional investor has found a neglected discount stock, others will begin to add the stock to their portfolios.

As the examples considered above show, it may take a year or two before any particular discount stock in the shadows gets the notice it deserves. If one invests in a stock in the deepest shadows, one may have to be patient for several years before being fully rewarded. Of course, one might find discount stocks on the edge of the shadows. If so, profiting from the stock's movement into institutional popularity will not take as long. However, in general, investors should be willing to wait at least several months for a stock to move completely from the shadows into the investment spotlight.

After moving into the spotlight, the security no longer has a place in a neglected-stock portfolio, and the question is whether the stock should be sold off. Here again, the decision cannot be made by using technical analysis of the popularity flow alone. The timing of shadow investment decisions should reflect both technical and fundamental analysis in the context of the investor's or manager's overall portfolio strategy. The latter is the topic of Chapters 9 and 10.

PART III

SHADOW INVESTMENT STRATEGIES

To reduce research costs, investors and managers need to reduce the number of eligible stocks, by as much pre-screening of the universe of securities as possible, before undertaking the intensive research described in Part II. With this in mind, Chapter 9 describes how to screen a universe of securities for a shadow stock opportunity set, to be used as a basis for the fundamental research needed to identify a true shadow portfolio. Chapter 10 then discusses the appropriate size of a shadow portfolio and how the latter can be integrated into a larger portfolio.

9

SCREENING
FOR A SHADOW
OPPORTUNITY SET

How can a series of screens be employed to identify an opportunity set of shadow stocks? To reduce the subsequent need for intensive research, the screens discussed in this chapter are designed to go as far as possible toward capturing some of the key factors discussed in Part II. The discussion includes consideration of the appropriate mix between screening and fundamental research.

OBJECTIVES AND CONSTRAINTS

No single investor can research all the stocks in the shadows. There are not enough hours in the day for an individual investor to do a thorough analysis on all stocks, of the type discussed in Part II. Recognizing this constraint, the investor must pare the opportunity set down to a manageable size. Screening is the most effective way of doing so. Screening can best be described as a systematic whittling down of the universe of stocks. In the end, the screened opportunity set is composed of stocks that satisfy objectives and constraints imposed by the individual needs of the investor.

All investors venturing into the shadows must decide how deep they want to go. Staying on the periphery of the shadows allows investors to benefit from some of the competitive advantage available from the 80/20 rule without seriously complicating the process of fundamental research. Venturing deep into the shadows, investors will have a greater comparative advantage, but will have to expend more effort on fundamental research.

To the extent that it is possible, screening is a viable complement to fundamental research in the shadows. Owing to its time efficiency, investors should utilize screening to its fullest extent prior to doing the necessary fundamental analysis on their investments. It must be emphasized, however, that screening cannot substitute for the fundamental analysis described in Part II. Rather, it can be employed to make investing in the shadows operationally efficient.

How much screening and research should be undertaken depends on the investor's objectives and constraints. No two investors will have exactly the same objectives and constraints. For example, institutional investors are less sensitive to fundamental research and are more sensitive to the riskiness of their portfolio. Individual investors, who have less time and expertise in fundamental methods, must limit the amount of fundamental research and may be less concerned with risk considerations. On moving into the shadows, the investor must first determine the level of shadow risk that is acceptable, giving careful consideration to its effect on fundamental research. Second, the investment horizon, and third, the liquidity needs must be established, because these are critical to success in the shadows.

Horizon is important, because the return on neglected stocks is strongly dependent on how much time is allowed for the passage from the shadows to the spotlight. Investors or managers with short horizons are exposed to greater risk of low returns in the shadows, since they may have to sell before the popularity flow materializes. It is imperative, therefore, that the shadow opportunity set be selected and researched with the implications of the horizon objective clearly in mind.

Liquidity constraints are also important, because many shadow stocks have low market capitalizations and are infrequently traded. Investors or institutions, with frequent liquidity needs, are thus exposed to greater risk in the shadows, since they may have to liquidate their holdings by selling into a thin market. These investors may wish to concentrate on the larger capitalization stocks often found in the periphery.

Taken together, risk, horizon, and liquidity objectives help determine the appropriate mix of screening and research. An institutional investor, for example, with low risk tolerance, short horizon, and high liquidity needs, can satisfy these objectives in the shadows only by using highly conservative screening, plus intensive security research on the resulting opportunity set. By contrast, an individual investor with high risk tolerance, long horizon, and low liquidity constraints can afford to screen much more aggressively, and limit the amount of research.

TRADE-OFFS IN THE SHADOWS

The trade-off between investment risk and total research effort on the one hand, and screening on the other hand, for a typical institutional or individual investor is depicted in Figure 9.1. The vertical axis shows the amount of total research engaged in by the investor. On the horizontal axis the amount of screening is measured. The curved lines in Figure 9.1 represent different levels of investment risk, with higher risk closer to the bottom of the graph and lower risk further up.

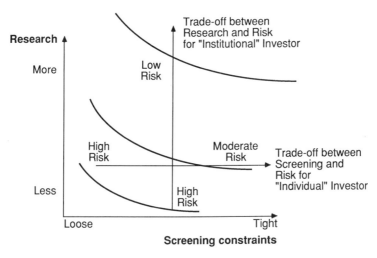

Figure 9.1   Trade-off between shadow risk and screening versus research.

Investors can move from one risk level to another by altering the mix of research and screening. If only one of these, either research or screening, is changed at a time, then the risk varies along the paths depicted by the crossing vertical and horizontal lines in the figure. Different types of investors, because of constraints imposed by ability and external factors, will find themselves positioned on different risk trade-off paths.

Individual investors often have limited resources, especially with respect to the time that can be devoted to in-depth security research. As a result, the typical individual investor faces the trade-off depicted by the horizontal arrow in Figure 9.1. If the investor's research effort is limited and, therefore, more or less constant, the risk exposure is determined by the kind of screening employed. Individuals should determine their research commitment, horizon, and liquidity objectives, and then use the intensity of screening to obtain the desired risk exposure. Keeping security research constant will limit the individual investor's ability to reduce risk exposure. Screening cannot substitute for security research. Therefore, investors who engage in little research, as in the case of the individual investor, will not be able to reduce their risk exposure below a moderate risk level.

Institutional investors face a different set of problems. They have to manage several portfolios at once, with clients looking over their shoulder. The needs and objectives of the clients often place well-defined constraints on the type of investments the portfolio manager can entertain. As a result, portfolio managers face screening constraints; they are limited in how far they can go into the shadows. With ample resources for fundamental research, the typical institutional manager faces a trade-off between shadow risk and security research best depicted diagramatically by the vertical arrow in Figure 9.1. After employing screening to satisfy customer-imposed horizon and liquidity constraints, managers can use security research to reduce the remaining shadow risk to a level acceptable to the client.

From this discussion it is apparent that the screening component of the risk trade-off faced by the individual or institution is highly dependent on the investor's objectives and constraints. At one extreme there are highly conservative investors; most institutions fall into this group. At the other extreme there are highly aggressive investors, with venture capitalists being the most aggressive of this group. The screening techniques that might be employed by these two extreme classes of investors are illustrated in the next section.

Most investors will find that they fall somewhere in between highly aggressive and highly conservative. In this case the investor may choose to mix the screening techniques to some extent. The precise mix is determined by the investor's risk tolerance in conjunction with an assessment of the total research time that can be expended. The analysis which follows could not hope to illustrate all the possible combinations. Therefore, for the sake of expediency, we will discuss only the two extremes corresponding to an aggressive and conservative investor, and allow individuals and institutions to position themselves wherever they feel comfortable.

Although not exhaustive, five different types of screens will be considered, each corresponding to one of the five chapters in Part II. In addition, supplementary diagrams are included with each set of screens to illustrate the effect of the screening process.

SCREENING FOR NEGLECT

Locating stocks in the shadows requires the screening of large numbers of stocks, which is most efficiently done with the aid of the computerized screening services discussed in Chapter 4. What distinguishes an aggressive from a conservative approach in the discovery of neglected firms is the cut-off point in terms of the number of analysts following the stock, or institutions holding shares. To obtain a neglected opportunity set, an aggressive individual might use the following cutoff points:

AGGRESSIVE APPROACH TO IDENTIFICATION

1. Eliminate all stocks with any analyst coverage.
2. Eliminate any stock which has more than five institutions holding shares.
3. Eliminate any stock which has more than five percent of its outstanding market value of equity held by institutions.

The most appropriate cutoff points depend on how far the investor wants to go into the shadows. The cutoffs used above, which are illustrative rather than prescriptive, usually generate an opportunity set of several hundred neglected stocks. The actual number of stocks isolated by any set of neglect screens varies with the state of the market. The attention of analysts and institutions differs not only across companies, but over time with respect to the market as a whole. The shadows lengthen during bear markets, for example, when there are many more neglected firms than during bull markets, because there is less analyst and institutional activity in the market as a whole.

As an aside, note that the order in which the universe of stocks is screened for neglect is unimportant. Whatever the order, the screening process selects only those stocks which satisfy all of the criteria used. This means that the screens can be employed in a sequence that reduces the associated cost. Depending on the data bases, it may be most expensive to screen for analyst attention. If so, it will be more economical to screen first for institutional holdings and percentage ownership, to reduce the size of the universe that subsequently must be screened for analyst attention.

Data bases, of course, completely eliminate the possibility of picking up new ventures, the most neglected stocks in the heart of the shadows. There is a world of difference between most new ventures and the companies listed on computerized data bases. The latter require at least some company history before going through the expense of reporting data on the stock. As a result, the stocks in the data bases are somewhat less risky, because they are beyond the critical first year or two of a new firm's life. By focusing on listed companies, one effectively screens out the extremely high risk/high return new ventures before even starting the screening process.

Of course, investors and managers can still try to identify isolated new venture stocks by employing the "wide-awake" approach mentioned in Chapter 8. New ventures frequently offer the most exciting possibilities. In the do-it-yourself mode, investors are surrounded by clues to possible profit opportunities in the market. All that is needed is sufficient awareness to recognize the clues when they present themselves. For instance, a new cordless telephone that all one's neighbors are buying, or a new series of integrated office software packages that are receiving rave reviews, or a new chain of off-the-shelf furniture distributors that is attracting droves of young customers, all are worth following up to see if they are publicly traded. If the identified company is not on any of the data bases, one may have something really exciting in one's investment sights.

By contrast to the aggressive individual, new ventures are out of the question for the conservative institution. If the latter wants to incorporate neglected stocks into its portfolio, it might employ the following screening criteria:

CONSERVATIVE APPROACH TO IDENTIFICATION

1. Eliminate all stocks with no analysts, as well as those with more than three analysts following the company.
2. Eliminate all stocks with 10 or more institutional shareholders.
3. Eliminate all stocks with more than 10 percent of their current outstanding market value of equity owned by institutions.

These criteria will isolate a set of moderately neglected stocks which should be accessible to most institutions whose risk, horizon, and liquidity objectives do not exclude shadow investment altogether.

Figure 9.2 illustrates the screening process for neglect in a diagramatic form. The vertical lines cover that part of the universe of stocks that has been eliminated by the screening process. On the left side of the exhibit the aggressive investor screens out all stocks

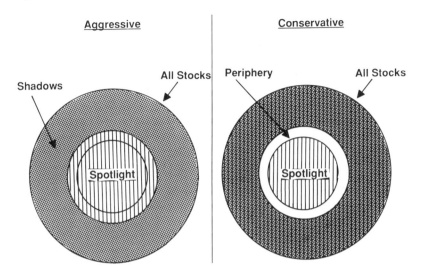

Figure 9.2   Screening for neglect.

not in the shadows. This includes stocks in the spotlight as well as those on the periphery. On the right of the exhibit the conservative investor screens out all stocks not in the periphery. In contrast to the aggressive investor, the conservative investor eliminates all stocks in the deep shadows as well as the spotlight.

SCREENING FOR LEMONS

The next step in the screening process is to eliminate as many losers as possible from the neglected opportunity set. Both numerical and judgmental approaches to the assessment of bankruptcy risk were discussed in Chapter 5. The numerical approaches lend themselves to incorporation in the screening procedures, whereas the judgmental methods should be included in the intensive research on the resulting opportunity set. The numerical ratio indicators of bankruptcy are the cash flow/total debt ratio and the return on assets.

An aggressive individual might decide to use a very loose screen for bankruptcy to avoid eliminating some of the most promising shadow stocks. Companies in a turnaround phase, like Chrysler in 1980, would not make it through a tight bankruptcy screen. Yet, if the turnaround is successful, they frequently make the ranks of the highest percentage gainers. Of course, the other side of the coin is the high risk of including some real lemons in the shadow portfolio.

AGGRESSIVE BANKRUPTCY SCREEN

1. Eliminate companies with three years of consecutive negative and declining negative EPS. (When available, use next year's EPS estimate as one of the three years of EPS under scrutiny.)

On the other hand, a conservative institution would definitely want to screen out possible bankruptcy candidates with a tighter screen. An appropriate set of criteria would be the following:

CONSERVATIVE BANKRUPTCY SCREEN

1. Eliminate those companies with cash flow/total debt ratios greater than the inverse of their average debt maturities, or a cut-off point of the investor's choice.
2. Eliminate those companies with return on assets (before taxes) less than the current interest rate on the company's debt.
3. Eliminate companies with three years of consecutive negative EPS. (When available, use next year's EPS estimate as one of the three years of EPS under scrutiny.)

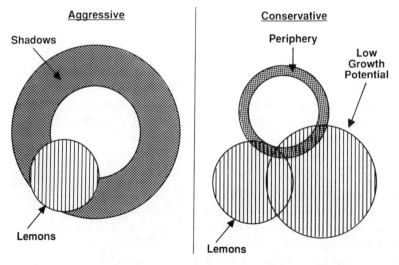

Figure 9.3   Screening for lemons and potential.

The rationale behind these criteria is given in Chapter 5. At this point, suffice it to say that the combination of these screens will help minimize the probability of investing in companies that are likely to have financial problems in the near future.

Figure 9.3 depicts the continuing screening process. For the aggressive investor the bankruptcy screen is looser than for the conservative investor and therefore eliminates proportionately fewer securities. The opportunity sets that remain after the bankruptcy screen are depicted by the areas in the shadows and the periphery, respectively, that are not crossed out.

SCREENING FOR POTENTIAL

Having reduced the downside risk component of the shadow opportunity set, one can now concentrate on trying to identify stocks with the earnings potential needed to emerge from the shadows. How can the neglected firms with real potential be selected? There's no apparent reason why the earnings shouldn't remain flat and the stocks continue to be neglected and ignored, perennial wallflowers, never in the limelight, hence the need to screen for earnings potential or growth. (A complete analysis of potential requires the kind of fundamental research discussed in Chapter 6.)

At least two variations of a potential screen based on earnings growth are possible, either used exclusively or in tandem. The first ranks the remaining stocks in the opportunity set in terms of their year-on-year quarterly earnings growth and screens out those with earnings growth less than that of the market as a whole. The disadvantage of this screen is its historical perspective and resulting tendency to eliminate high-potential turnaround stocks; the advantage is its corresponding conservatism. The second growth screen compares the last year's EPS to the analysts' EPS forecast for the next year and screens out stocks with declining EPS expectations. The advantage of this screen is its forward-looking nature. However, it is applicable only to stocks followed by at least one analyst.

The aggressive individual cannot use the second growth screen, because the corresponding aggressive opportunity set has already excluded stocks followed by analysts. The first growth screen is too historical in orientation for the objectives of this kind of investor.

AGGRESSIVE SCREEN FOR POTENTIAL

1. To avoid eliminating the stocks with truly exciting potential, do not screen for historical growth.

By contrast, a very conservative institution might apply both growth screens mentioned above, whereas a somewhat less conservative institution might only utilize the second one.

CONSERVATIVE SCREEN FOR POTENTIAL

1. Screen out stocks with year-on-year quarterly earnings growth less than that of the market as a whole.
2. Screen out stocks with analyst-forecasted EPS less than last year's EPS.

The impact of the potential screen on the conservative opportunity set is illustrated in Figure 9.3 by the additional crossed-out area.

SCREENING FOR DISCOUNTS

For all investors, the ultimate objective is to identify stocks in the opportunity set which are selling at a true discount. To do so requires a comparison between the company's potential value and its current price. Even neglected firms can be overvalued. Despite the relative lack of analysts' and institutional attention, investors and managers are never quite alone in the shadows. Others may have discovered the potential of a neglected stock beforehand, and the price might already have been bid up. The stock may be on its way out of the shadows. What is needed, therefore, is a screen for discount stocks, to identify those that are truly undervalued.

The advantages and disadvantages of statistically based valuation models incorporating risk and growth were discussed in Chapter 7. There is no obvious reason why the bankruptcy and potential screens could not be collapsed into a single screen for discount stocks based on a statistical P/E valuation model. This would be most appropriate for the conservative institution interested in the shadow periphery. Unfortunately for the aggressive individual in the deep shadows, the necessary risk and growth data would be very difficult to obtain, for a large set of neglected stocks.

Instead of employing a statistical model, one can screen the P/E ratios in the opportunity set directly and reject as overrated all those stocks with P/E ratios greater than the market average. Apart from its simplicity, an advantage of this screen is that it represents the essence of the original contrarian strategy. Historically it has resulted in portfolios with superior returns, all by itself (see Chapter 2). A disadvantage is the possibility again of eliminating turn-around stocks with low current EPS and, hence, an artificially high P/E ratio.

For companies with a recent deficit, the P/E ratio based on historical earnings is meaningless. To screen stocks with a deficit for possible overvaluation, a weak substitute for the P/E ratio is provided by the position of the current price in the range between its 52-week high and low. The relative price position is expressed in terms of the current price minus the low, divided by the high price minus the low. When this price position statistic is greater than 0.5 for a stock with a deficit—that is, when the current price is closer to the 52-week high than the low—the security might be classified as overrated.

Appropriate screening criteria to identify possible discount stocks would be the following:

AGGRESSIVE SCREEN FOR DISCOUNTS

1. For stocks without recent deficits, select those with a P/E ratio (based on current earnings) that is less than 0.75 the market's average P/E.
2. For stocks with recent deficits, select those with a relative price position of less than 0.5.

CONSERVATIVE SCREEN FOR DISCOUNTS

1. Select stocks with a P/E ratio less than the market's average P/E.

The impact of the discount screen is depicted in Figure 9.4 by the crossed-out areas associated with the elimination of high P/E stocks for the conservative investor and high plus medium P/E stocks for the aggressive investor.

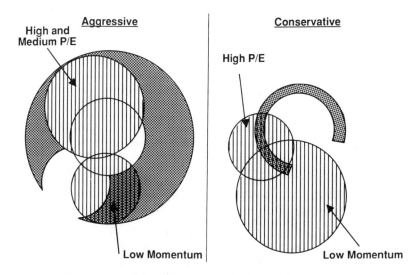

Figure 9.4   Screening for discounts and momentum.

SCREENING FOR POPULARITY MOMENTUM

Even true discount stocks may remain neglected for long periods, before their potential is recognized and they pick up momentum for a move into the spotlight. Chapter 8 discussed several indicators of a stock's popularity within the investment community. One or more of these can be used to screen the opportunity set for those discount stocks which are displaying momentum in terms of increasing popularity. But the ultimate measure of momentum, the one that really matters in terms of investment return, is the stock's price. Recent price movement, combined with rising analyst and institutional interest, provides an appropriate screen for momentum.

For the aggressive individual, however, this combined screen may be too conservative. Aggressive investors would prefer to catch the stock while it is still in the deep shadows. The time lags associated with data on analyst and institutional following are too conservative for the aggressive investor, because they may screen out stocks with price momentum. An aggressive approach, therefore, might employ the screen below.

AGGRESSIVE SCREEN FOR MOMENTUM

1. Select stocks with a trend of increasingly positive price changes over the last three months.

By contrast, a conservative institution would want to avoid investing in a discount stock which remains a shadows wallflower for a long period, neglected by analysts and institutions. Hence, a conservative approach might use the criteria mentioned below to screen for momentum.

CONSERVATIVE SCREEN FOR MOMENTUM

1. Select stocks with a trend of increasingly positive price changes over the last three months.
2. Select stocks with an increasing number of institutional holdings over the last three months.
3. Select stocks with an increase in the number of analysts over the last three months.

The addition of the momentum screen to the four types of screens discussed above will produce shadow opportunity sets of possible discount stocks corresponding to the objectives of either the aggressive or conservative investor, as depicted in Figure 9.4.

THE LIMITS OF SCREENING

The objective of the screening process was to reduce the number of stocks in the shadow opportunity set. As can be seen from Figure 9.4, there will be more stocks in an aggressive loosely screened opportunity set than in a conservative tightly screened one. What are the implications for the fundamental research that must follow screening? To find out whether the stocks in the shadow opportunity set are true discount stocks, the investor or portfolio manager cannot avoid the intensive security research described in Chapters 5, 6, and 7.

For a given amount of resources devoted to security research, much more can be done per stock by the conservative investor who employs tight screens, because there are fewer stocks in the opportunity set. The aggressive investor must spread the same resources over a larger number of stocks. This exposes the aggressive investor to higher risk, due to the greater difficulty in discriminating between the lemons and discounts in the shadow opportunity set.

The only way for an investor to reduce risk exposure to a low level and improve the discriminating power between lemons and discounts is to increase the resources allocated to fundamental research. For an institutional investor, this is no problem, since the resources for research can easily be increased. In effect, as far as resources go, institutional investors can position themselves anywhere on the research-screening map. As mentioned earlier, however, they frequently have constraints imposed by their clients and/ or charter that force them to engage in at least a moderate level of screening.

For the individual investor, on the other hand, the resource constraint tends to be paramount. The only way of achieving a lower risk level is to apply a greater research effort to each stock. This can be achieved by restricting attention to an arbitrary subset of the screened stocks, or by screening tightly to reduce the opportunity set to a manageable number of stocks. The problem is that this limits the possibilities for diversification. For the conservative individual, therefore, tight screening is important and careful fundamental research is indispensable if the shadow risk exposure is to be contained.

Another possible alternative available to individual investors is to turn to professional services specifically designed to tap into the superior returns available in the shadows. For those investors who wish to maintain active control of their investments, there is a newsletter that identifies promising shadow stocks. The Generic Stock Investment Service is available by writing to P.O. Box 6567, Ithaca, NY 14851. Those investors who would rather not take an active role can invest in a shadow stock mutual fund. Examples of such funds are the Philadelphia Investment Management Group and Fidelity's OTC Fund.

After identification of the true discount stocks in the shadow opportunity set, a decision must be made on when and how much to invest in the shadows. These topics are addressed in the next chapter.

10

PUTTING A PORTFOLIO MIX TOGETHER

What percentage of a portfolio should be invested in the shadows and how much in each neglected stock? Is more or less diversification needed? This final chapter provides guidelines for the construction and maintenance of a shadow investment portfolio.

COMPOSITION OF SHADOW PORTFOLIO

How much should be invested in each of the discount stocks identified by the screening and research process? Both simple and more complex guidelines are available. Let us first consider two well-known simple rules for portfolio composition: the equally weighted and the value weighted rules.

Simple Diversification Rules

In an equally weighted portfolio, an equal dollar amount is invested in each stock. An equally weighted portfolio clearly favors the smaller companies, because each of them comprises as much of the portfolio as a large company. In general, in an equally weighted portfolio, the investor is trading off larger firm diversification for the hoped-for higher returns associated with smaller firms. But in the shadows, this is usually not the case. Chapter 2 demonstrated that neglected stocks tend to perform better than researched stocks regardless of whether they are large or small. In other words, there is no particular benefit to be obtained in the shadows by investing equally in small and large discount stocks. The investor might be better off going for the greater diversification associated with the larger discount stocks.

More emphasis can be given to the larger discount stocks by using the value-weighted composition rule. In a value-weighted portfolio the amounts invested vary according to the market capitalizations of the stocks. By giving more weight to the larger stocks in the shadow opportunity set, the investor has a better chance of getting whatever diversification is available in the shadows, without sacrificing the superior returns on discount stocks.

More complete shadow diversification might involve investing smaller amounts in many shadow stocks on a value-weighted basis. The stocks might be selected using aggressive loose screening. The number of stocks may make it difficult to perform intensive fundamental research on each of the stocks. Diversification plus inclusion in a larger portfolio, therefore, is needed to control the risk. A neglected stock fund, like those discussed at the end of Chapter 9, might provide the vehicle for such an approach. By contrast less complete diversification might involve investing larger, equal amounts in fewer shadow stocks, while relying on conservative tight screening and intensive fundamental research with inclusion in a larger portfolio to contain the risk.

The disadvantage of these rules is that they completely ignore the relative performance of the stocks in the opportunity set. Not all discount stocks have the same potential. Other things being equal, rational investors prefer to invest more in the securities with the greater return potential. The value-weighted rule is most useful, therefore, when it is difficult to make an estimate with any confidence about the future performance of a shadow stock and the investor is relying on diversification and screening rather than research to contain the risk.

Quantitative Portfolio Composition

A more quantitative approach to portfolio composition can be employed when the fundamental research produces estimates of systematic risk and future return on the discount stocks in the shadow opportunity set. Elton, Gruber, and Padberg (EGP) have developed a relatively simple ranking device to determine an optimal portfolio mix, based on excess return per unit of systematic risk. (See Chapter 2 for the definition of excess return.) The ranking system incorporates stocks into the portfolio primarily on the basis of the stock's excess return per unit of systematic risk.

Implementation of the ranking method involves four relatively simple steps. First, on the basis of fundamental research, the excess return to beta index is calculated for each stock in the opportunity set. The stocks are then ranked by excess return to beta from the highest to the lowest. The ranking represents the desirability of inclusion in the portfolio. Second, performance standards are calculated for each stock in combination with those higher up the ranking. Third, all stocks with excess return to beta greater than the corresponding performance standard are selected for inclusion in the optimal portfolio. Fourth, the percentage invested in each security is calculated, mainly on the basis of the stock's return variance and the difference between the stock's excess return to beta and its performance standard.

EGP's ranking method maximizes the excess portfolio return per unit of risk, relative to the risk free T-bill rate. The investor's risk preferences are assumed to be satisfied via investment in the optimal portfolio plus appropriate borrowing or lending. Thus, the ranking system lends itself to the selection of country shadow portfolios, if desired, each tied to a different national risk-free rate.

For shadow portfolio selection, the ranking system has the advantage of already having been adapted to the new beta incorporating shadow risk. Robert Pari and Son-Nan Chen adapted the ranking system to the new beta and then applied the modified procedure to a trial sample of ten firms, five with high shadow risk and five with low shadow risk, as measured by the variation in analysts forecasts. The results are shown in Table 10.1.

The first interesting feature in the data is the size of some of the companies with high shadow risk in the form of high analyst uncertainty (DEC, Champion, Getty Oil, Chrysler). Although uncertainty is not the same as neglect, the two are highly correlated, which demonstrates once again that the information shadows may be populated by otherwise surprisingly well-known companies.

The reward-to-risk ratio reflects the historical mean monthly return minus the risk free T-bill rate divided by the new beta, with the latter calculated as in Chapter 5. Allowing for analyst uncertainty, only the first five of the stocks make it into the optimal portfolio with reward-to-risk ratios exceeding their performance standard. Comparison of the last two columns shows that the inclusion of shadow risk in the form of analyst uncertainty reduces the number of securities in the optimal portfolio from nine to six. Three of the five companies with high shadow risk in the form of analyst uncertainty are excluded from the portfolio. The optimal weights of the selected stocks also change significantly. Securities accompanied by less analyst uncertainty, like Federal Express, are weighted more heavily compared with those closer to the shadows with more uncertainty, like Getty Oil.

As Pari and Chen point out, it is dangerous to generalize from only one sample of ten firms. Nevertheless, when short sales are excluded, as in this example, one can say that shadow risk tends to reduce the number of holdings in the optimal portfolio. The in-

TABLE 10.1 Impact of Shadow Risk on Portfolio Composition

1979–1983 Security	Coefficient of Variation in Analysts' Forecasts	Reward-to-Risk Ratio	Performance Standard	Portfolio Weights	
				With Shadow Risk	Without Shadow Risk
Federal Express	.025	.0201	.0010	23.2%	17.9%
General Foods	.014	.0128	.0014	14.2	11.5
Ametek	.072	.0120	.0032	36.5	32.9
Chrysler	.268	.0084	.0036	4.4	5.3
Exxon	.031	.0083	.0042	18.4	18.0
Getty Oil	.222	.0054	.0045	3.3	10.4
Datapoint	.175	.0037	.0045	0.0	1.9
Eastman Kodak	.050	.0036	.0046	0.0	1.5
Champion Sparkplug	.263	.0012	.0040	0.0	0.6
Digital Equipment	.255	.0006	.0033	0.0	0.0

Source: Robert Pari and S. Chen, "Estimation Risk and Optimal Portfolios," *Journal of Portfolio Management,* Fall 1985. Reprinted with permission.

corporation of the variance in analysts' forecasts increases the new beta, relative to the historical beta, thereby lowering the reward-to-risk ratio. The key message is that risk-averse investors should avoid securities whose "excess returns do not justify the additional exposure to (shadow) risk."

However, a reminder is in order here. The analysts' forecast variance is needed to estimate a new beta, in order to compute the reward-to-risk ratio in Table 10.1. The best that can be done in the deep shadows is to estimate beta by extrapolation from the spotlight. (See Chapters 5 and 7.) More importantly, the example in Table 10.1 is based on historical returns that cannot capture the possibility of an impending shift from the shadows into the spotlight. Historical returns were used to illustrate the impact of shadow risk on portfolio composition, rather than as an example of what should be done to put together a shadow portfolio in practice. For the latter, fundamental research is required to get a future return estimate that improves on what is built into the existing market price.

AMOUNT OF INVESTMENT IN THE SHADOWS

How much of a total portfolio should be in the shadows? The answer depends on two factors: first, the overall return and risk characteristics of the shadow portfolio selected by the screening, research, and portfolio composition process, and second, the investor's risk tolerance. Other constraints affecting the investor are embedded in the screening process described in Chapter 9.

With respect to the risk of the shadow portfolio, it is important to recall the limits to the diversification of company-specific risk in the shadows. Even a diversified shadow portfolio of small firms may be exposed to more total risk than a single large diversified company in the spotlight. Thus, conservative investors or institutions will violate their tolerance for risk if they invest in the shadows exclusively. Although by definition aggressive investors have greater risk tolerance, they too should be wary of exclusive investment in the shadows. This is especially the case if the shadow portfolio has been selected primarily by screening with relatively little fundamental research. In most cases, therefore, the shadow portfolio has to be incorporated into a larger portfolio to obtain the desired diversification.

Perhaps the simplest approach to deciding how much should be invested in the shadows lies in the notion of risk capital. The latter represents funds that the investor or manager can afford to lose without endangering the longer-run performance of the portfolio. Needless to say, this is a somewhat vague notion. In general, risk capital represents funds that the investor is willing to invest at high risk in pursuit of a higher return. Given the greater risk in the shadows, the percentage of risk capital may, therefore, be used as a rough indicator of how much might be invested in the shadows.

For a more precise answer to the question, a quantitative portfolio analysis technique can be employed. Unfortunately, such analyses tend to be complex and dependent on historical data. The quantitative approaches are based on the quadratic programming approach introduced by Harry Markowitz in 1952. His method has never really made the transition into the practitioner's tool kit, owing to the complexity of the data needed: a huge number of expected returns, variances, and correlation coefficients have to be estimated before the method can be implemented. It is a rare analyst who can comfortably predict the future correlation coefficients between all the stocks in a particular decision set. Such prediction is especially difficult because historical correlation coefficients are not a good guide to future correlation between individual securities.

In a recent attempt at a practical application of the quadratic programming approach, William Sharpe has employed an average of the more stable past correlation relationships, not between individual securities, but between industry, country, and fund indices. These include equity on the major world stock exchanges, bonds, real estate, metals, foreign exchange, and even a small firm fund. The correlation between indices tends to be much more stable over time than the correlation between individual securities—hence their usefulness in programmed portfolio optimization. Sharpe asks the investor to specify the level of risk tolerance in terms of variance per unit of return, by indicating preferences for different mixes of stocks and bonds, based on their performance between 1926 and 1961. Given the desired risk tolerance, the program then produces a portfolio of the asset categories selected with an overall risk and return that equals the investor's risk tolerance.

Since Sharpe's program allows the introduction of "data from other sources," there is no technical reason why the historical returns on shadow stocks cannot be added to the existing data base. Unfortunately, given the limitations of historical data in the shadows, the inclusion of individual shadow stock returns is not advisable. The potential transition from the shadows to the spotlight is one of the fundamental attractions of shadow investment that cannot be captured with historical returns. The same is true of shadow risk.

Sharpe's quadratic programming model is best suited to the allocation of a large institutional portfolio across the broad asset categories captured by the indices in the data base. The incorporation of individual shadow securities is out of place in this context. It violates the relative stability of the index data. Much more advisable is first to compose a shadow portfolio, and then to introduce this portfolio as a whole into Sharpe's program in much the same way as the small firm fund. Given the desired risk tolerance, the program would then solve for how much of the investor's funds should have been in the shadows historically. In so far as it depends on historical data, however, the best that can be hoped for from the program is a ballpark indication of how much should be invested in the shadows in the future.

PORTFOLIO MAINTENANCE

Once a portfolio has been put together, it has to be maintained. Although successful shadow investment is typically associated with a long horizon, portfolio maintenance, albeit less frequent, is still necessary. As has been the case for most of the methods discussed in this book, there are basically two complementary approaches to portfolio maintenance, one quantitative and the other qualitative.

If quantitative return and risk projections are available, the EGP ranking method can be used to decide when to invest and divest. The ranking method prescribes that stocks be bought for inclusion in the portfolio when their reward-to-risk ratio exceeds the performance standard. When neglected stocks begin to move into the spotlight, their reward-to-risk ratio rises automatically. As more information becomes available, analyst uncertainty tends to decline and with it, the new beta. At the same time, the increasing analysts' attention usually generates a rising price and hence increasing return. Both together, the declining beta and rising price push up the reward-to-risk ratio, creating a buy signal when it passes the performance standard. Conversely, once a stock is in the spotlight, there is little further reduction in informational uncertainty. As a result, the new beta tends to stabilize. Consequently, any significant reduction in projected returns which lowers the reward-to-risk ratio below the performance standard constitutes a sell signal.

However, why would investors and managers want to wait for a buy or sell signal from the ranking system that will only occur once the stock is well on its way into the spotlight? At this stage, most of the price movement may be history. The aim should be to buy just before the stock begins to attract attention, or at least before it has attracted too much attention. The whole idea is to catch the popularity flow toward a promising shadow stock before it gathers momentum, and ride the flow until it changes direction.

Qualitative Portfolio Maintenance

The qualitative approach to portfolio maintenance relies on monitoring popularity, as described in Chapter 8. By monitoring the attention of analysts and the interest of institutions, the investor or manager can anticipate changes in the reward-to-risk ratio, without having to await their confirmation in the ex post ratio itself. One approach might be to invest in a shadow stock when the number of institutional holdings increases to above 10, say, or when the first analysts begin to follow the stock. The important point is not so much the number of institutions or analysts, which depends on whether an aggressive or conservative approach is being adopted, but rather their use as in indication of a positive change in sentiment. A noticeable increase in the number of institutions or analysts represents a buy signal.

As an example of the timing decision in the shadows, consider the pattern of I/B/E/S analyst following, institutional holdings, and share price, for Commodore International, an emerging computer stock in the early 1980s. See Table 10.2.

The analysis presented in Chapters 5, 6, and 7 suggested that Commodore International was undervalued at the end of 1980. At that point Commodore was covered by only one analyst and held by nine institutions. According to the criteria established earlier,

TABLE 10.2   Example of Shadow Investment Timing
Based on Shifting Popularity

	Institutional* Holding[1]	Number of Analysts[2]	Share Price[3]
October 1980	9	1	11.41
January 1981	16	4	13.21
June 1981	23	7	16.00
May 1982	39	11	17.43
November 1982	62	12	29.56
January 1983	75	13	35.24
June 1983	86	15	58.25
September 1983	109	14	45.00
March 1984	98	13	33.25
December 1984	90	11	24.37
June 1985	78	10	8.62

*All numbers represent end of month values.

[1]*Source:* S&P Stock Guide

[2]*Source:* I/B/E/S Monthly Comments

[3]*Source:* Center for Research in Security Prices

Commodore International represented a strong buy opportunity. Between October 1980 and June 1983 the level of analyst coverage rose to 15 and the number of institutions holding the company's stock increased to 86. During the same period Commodore's stock price rose from $11.41 per share to $58.25, more than a 500% rise. This exhibits the popularity flow in action.

Once shadow stocks are in the portfolio, they must be monitored together with the stocks in the backup opportunity set, not only for changes in the reward-to-risk ratio, but also for shifts in analyst attention. The purpose is to ride the popularity flow as long as possible. Owing to the judgment involved, however, divesting from the shadows is often much more difficult than investing. It is relatively easy to divest when things have gone well, more or less according to plan. If the rise in the reward-to-risk ratio of a neglected stock continues until the stock becomes highly researched, and possibly beyond, taking a capital gain when the popularity flow ebbs is a pleasant exercise.

But if the reward-to-risk momentum reverses itself after investment, or if the popularity flow never materializes and the stock languishes in neglect, then what? This is when the discipline of a well-defined exiting strategy becomes critical. A strict exiting strategy is best defined within the context of one of the portfolio optimization models like the ranking system. The issue in the shadows, again, is whether the popularity flow can be used to sharpen the decision.

When the stock benefits from a wave of popularity, the investor will want to get the most out of it. Thus, if the price of the stock declines before it is fully in the spotlight, but the stock's potential based on fundamental research remains strong, it may be reasonable to remain invested in anticipation of a turnaround in the price trend. A good example is what happened to Commodore between November of 1981 and June of 1982, when the price first declined from $11 to $9 and then rose to $16, while the stock's popularity and potential remained intact. Similarly, if the stock is in the spotlight with continuing reward-to-risk momentum, there's no point in selling. The investor should exit, however, once the stock is fully in the spotlight; the potential has dissipated, and the corresponding reward-to-risk momentum is declining.

After June 1983 Commodore's situation started to change. The month after Commodore hit $58.25 per share one analyst dropped his coverage. By September, institutional sponsorship had peaked at 109. From that point on both institutional ownership and analyst coverage fell. As indicated in Table 10.2, Commodore's price dropped as well. Accordingly, the stock represented a strong sell situation.

The more difficult exiting decision occurs when, after an initial increase in price, the popularity flow does not materialize. The sell decisions, or lack of them, in this situation will separate the successful from the unsuccessful investors in neglected stocks. In the absence of a popularity flow, if either the stock's potential evaporates or the reward-to-risk momentum reverses itself, the stock should be sold. The successful investor will follow a well-defined exiting strategy dispassionately, without allowing emotion or intellectual pride to prevent timely divestment.

All this having been said, what remains is for the investor to make a move into the shadows. Before doing so, however, it is important to match the choice of the shadows depth with one's desire for active investment, a point highlighted in the concluding note.

CONCLUDING NOTE: TAKING THE PLUNGE

The fact that the opportunities in the shadows cannot be fully exploited without a good dose of judgment is a reflection of the entrepreneurial nature of the market for shadow information. In the full information of the spotlight, intense competition makes automatic investment rules economically attractive and reduces the opportunities for entrepreneurial gain to a minimum. By contrast, whether it is fundamental analysis to appraise a neglected stock's potential, or a form of technical analysis on the popularity flow for investment timing, the more profitable shadow decisions cannot be made automatically. The lack of information and concomitant uncertainty in the shadows both facilitate entrepreneurial gains from security research and necessitate judgment in its execution.

Thus, before plunging into the shadows, investors and managers must appraise their desire and aptitude for entrepreneurial activity in the information market. In the final analysis, it is the taste for information entrepreneurship which should determine how the investor matches his risk preference with the shadows. The deepest shadows can be successfully exploited only by dedicated and extremely aggressive information entrepreneurs, with the special combination of vision, ability, commitment, and patience to allow them to accept the challenges of the shadows for the rewards that follow.

Aggressive investors and managers might adopt a shadow strategy corresponding to the aggressive screening, research, and diversification approach outlined in Parts II and III. Creativity in both data accumulation and its subsequent analysis can provide managers with the competitive information edge which, if they are persistent and thoughtful, will allow them to exploit the undiscovered discount stocks, the cinderellas of the future. More conservative investors and managers, on the other hand, might adopt the corresponding conservative strategy outlined above. Very conservative managers, with little taste for information entrepreneurship, can still participate in the shadows by including a neglected stock fund when putting together their overall index portfolio.

Whatever their taste for information entrepreneurship, the bottom line is that investors with sufficient capital and managers who want greater returns cannot afford to ignore the shadows. In the spotlight, the best that can be done is to take a random walk down Wall Street with the averages. In order to outpace the averages, once must move into the shadows. The evidence is overwhelming and leaves virtually no doubt that the shadows offer the highest returns and the best opportunities for beating the averages. In investment, as in any other activity, those who distinguish themselves go beyond the limits of the well-known to explore the unknown, beyond the limits of the spotlight to invest in the shadows.

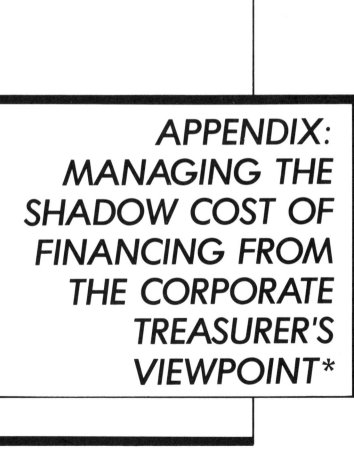

APPENDIX: MANAGING THE SHADOW COST OF FINANCING FROM THE CORPORATE TREASURER'S VIEWPOINT*

*Adapted from Paul Strebel, "Managing the Information Cost of Financing," *Columbia Journal of World Business* (Summer 1986).

In contrast to the three main parts of the book which take the perspective of the investor in the informational shadows, this appendix is written from the viewpoint of the financial manager of a neglected firm. Two types of shadow financing cost are identified: the scarce information premium, corresponding to the superior investor return on neglected firms, and the expectations gap, reflecting the frequent over- or undervaluation of shadow firms. The appendix focuses on how these information costs of financing can be reduced.

SHADOWS COST OF FINANCING

Higher financing costs are the mirror image of the superior returns on neglected firms in the shadows. The lack of information in the shadows and differences in the expectations of shadow investors can make a significant difference to the cost of capital. From the viewpoint of corporate treasurers in shadow firms, the difficulty of communicating all the relevant information to the financial markets makes the information possessed by management and potential financiers far from identical. Whereas the information that is easiest to communicate tends to be in numerical or financial form, the most useful information is frequently qualitative or intangible. Competitive considerations, moreover, often preclude disclosure of the most sensitive and, therefore, most relevant information. As a result, there is plenty of scope either for lack of information, or for differences in expectations to affect the price that financiers are willing to pay for a shadow firm's future cash flows.

Consider, for example, Novo Industrii A/S, a Danish pharmaceutical/biotech company, which was selling at six times earnings in the small shadows market of Copenhagen early in 1980. But its management knew that comparable companies were selling at 15 to 30 times earnings in the spotlight of the New York market. With a series of "road shows," followed by new issues in both London and New York, Novo first gained the attention of overseas investors, who then helped to change the expectations of the Danish market by arbitraging the multiple up to 17.

Another example, Pakhoed Holding N.V., a Dutch company, had a price-earnings ratio of 18 on the Amsterdam exchange in 1974, but was virtually unknown in the international financial community. An international public capital issue was ruled out. The company reached agreement with a group of prime quality banks for a U.S. $30 million multicurrency loan managed by the Banque Européenne de Crédit and Morgan Guaranty as a first step towards building its image in the international capital market. This was followed in 1976 by a greatly oversubscribed $25 million Eurobond issue managed by the Amsterdam-Rotterdam Bank N.V. and Morgan Stanley International.

By contrast with these shadow examples, in the spotlight virtually the same information is available to everyone. Managers cannot create value for their shareholders through financing, because the price offered for the company's cash flows is equal to their value. The smaller the informational differences between managers and financiers, the less the potential impact of financing on the firm's value. In this kind of environment, the choice of financing is practically irrelevant.

From the financial officer's point of view, there are two types of informational cost. The first is the "scarce information premium," which corresponds to the superior return on neglected firms that investors/financiers require as compensation for the uncertainty generated by lack of information in the shadows. The second, which may be either positive or negative, is associated with the "financial expectations gap" about the shadow company's prospects, which frequently exists between management and its advisors on the one hand, and the financial markets on the other. This expectations gap results in either under- or overvaluation of the shadow firm's equity.

Understanding the link between publicly available information and financing costs is the first step in the development of an appropriate action plan aimed at reducing these information costs. For example, does the company suffer from a lack of research attention on the part of the financial community, or from a distorted financial image, or both? In the event of a lack of attention, what are the financing implications? Should more financial, strategic, or product information perhaps be disclosed in an attempt to gain attention? In the event of a distorted financial image, can (should) financial marketing be used to close the expectations gap? (See Table A.1.)

The answers to these questions depend in part on where the company is located, in which country and capital market. It will be assumed that the company is sufficiently close to its target capital structure, and that the other factors affecting financing costs,

TABLE A.1   Reducing the Shadow Cost of Financing

IS THE PROBLEM:

(A) Lack of financier attention?
(B) Distorted financial image?

APPROACH (A): REDUCE THE SCARCE INFORMATION PREMIUM

(1) Use retained earnings
(2) Rely on old financial friends
(3) Attract attention

APPROACH (B): MANAGE THE EXPECTATIONS GAP

(1) Alter corporate strategy and expectations
(2) Focus image with financial marketing
(3) Exploit the expectations gap
(4) Arbitrage expectations across markets

such as taxes, bankruptcy, flexibility, and control, are more or less offsetting. Under these conditions information costs will be most likely to shape the financing decision, and the policy guidelines for reducing such costs will be most relevant.

REDUCING THE SCARCE INFORMATION PREMIUM

Companies neglected by analysts are often small or static, have low general visibility, and are unwilling to disclose inside information (see Chapter 1). As shown in Chapter 2, the phenomenon certainly is not unique to small firms. Even among the largest companies, some get virtually no attention at all.

To minimize the cost of financing associated with a lack of financial attention, neglected firms must either find a way of increasing their popularity, or of avoiding the financing premium associated with scarce information. An analysis of the possibilities open to a neglected company suggests, by a process of elimination, at least three different actions which management can take to avoid, or reduce the scarce information premium:

Use Retained Earnings

The information premium is lower for retained earnings than for other forms of financing. Management acts as a financial agent on behalf of the existing shareholders and, by definition, has more inside information than the agents of other potential investors or financing clienteles. To the extent that financial clienteles rely on intermediaries such as management, investment bankers, portfolio managers, and so on to act as agents for them, the existing shareholder clientele is better informed than other potential clienteles. As a result, retained earnings has a relatively low information cost of financing. Neglected companies in particular, therefore, should use this form of financing.

But retained earnings financing is affected by the dividend decision. Dividends should not be altered temporarily to reflect short-run financing requirements, because the reduction in the scarce information financing premium may be offset by the additional uncertainty created by a varying dividend signal.

Many firms are already aware of the lower cost of retained earnings. A good example is provided by Nestlé, which used part of its liquid reserve of U.S. $7 billion to help finance the takeover of Carnation for U.S. $3 billion. A recent statistical analysis of existing financial practice in the United States also found that retained earnings were a preferred form of financing. The results of this study were summarized as follows: "Don't use debt if the earnings flow is generous enough to make it unnecessary."

Rely on Old Financial Friends

Neglected companies can avoid much of the financing premium associated with scarce information by relying on the financiers who know them best. By the same token, the development of ongoing relationships with banking and other "private" sources of finance is critical.

Financial relationships that reduce the information premium take effort to develop. Because the financier has to learn and gradually build confidence in his information about the firm, its operations, products, and markets, such relationships cannot be developed overnight, but have to be nurtured over time. Bell Canada

Enterprises, for example, began studying and building relationships for international syndication a full five years before making their issue in June 1983.

Clearly, the more neglected or informationally naked the firm is in the public capital markets, the more important private financial relationships become, as a means of reducing the information cost of financing. Pakhoed's use of private international bank financing when it was unknown, prior to making a public Eurobond issue when it was better known, is a good illustration of this point.

Attract Attention

Small companies can reduce the scarce information premium by attracting attention. More attention results in more information being obtained by security analysts and made available to the financial community, thereby reducing the uncertainty associated with the anticipated return distribution.

Well-placed financial publicity has permitted many small firms to project themselves into the financial spotlight. The recent equity issues of small high-technology companies fall into this category. Some companies have used the introduction of new products to get a partial free ride in the media. It was mentioned in Chapter 3, for example, that Apple Computer uses extravaganzas "complete with glaring spotlights and loud music," to introduce new products to analysts and the press.

What is needed, in addition to favorable publicity, is an aggressive investment banker-cum-broker with access to a network of investors interested in speculative high-growth stocks. A typical example is the case of two entrepreneurs, who, with nothing other than a pending FCC application for a cordless telephone license, but with one highly publicized successful venture behind them and access to aggressive brokers, raised $2 million of over-the-counter equity.

However, the ability of smaller firms to move out of the financing shadows into the spotlight is constrained by their size. From the analysts' viewpoint, there is often not enough of a market for the securities of a small firm to pay for the cost of security research (except possibly at the time of a new issue, when underwriting fees come into play). Moreover, when the main financial marketing objective of small firms is merely favorable publicity, it is of dubious value, because the market discounts the publicity as such. As a result, there are limits to what small firms can do with financial marketing.

Even large companies, as we have seen, or whole industries may need to attract attention from time to time. This is illustrated by the case of the American do-it-yourself industry. Companies catering to the do-it-yourself market were not even recognized as an industry on Wall Street until Donald Davis of Stanley Works and others created the Do-It-Yourself Research Institute to promote the industry and develop research material. Stanley Works claims that 50 analysts are "consistently interested" in it, compared with 15 before the Institute started. Without ignoring the role of other factors, it is interesting to note that the price-earnings ratio of Stanley Works climbed from an average of 8 in 1980, before the Institute started, to 14.5 in 1982.

For most large companies, however, the investor relations effort is more a question of influencing the financial market's image of the company, than the market's awareness of its existence.

MANAGING THE EXPECTATIONS GAP

The obvious reaction to an apparently distorted financial image is some form of financial marketing. But before deciding on a financial marketing effort, management must determine what sort of financial image the company has: What kind of information has been getting through to the financial community? What kind of financial clienteles does the company have? Which of them has the most positive expectations about the firm's future? For companies listed in more than one market, can the differences between the clienteles be exploited, as Novo Industrii did when it capitalized on the far more bullish sentiment towards biotech stocks in New York relative to Copenhagen?

Before we consider possible differences between clienteles, the first question that must be answered is whether there is a gap between the perception of management and the financiers as a whole. If so, what should be done about it? For example, if the financial markets have a more pessimistic view of the company's prospects than management, financing costs look high from management's perspective, and vice versa. There is no way of knowing who will be more correct about a particular future—management or the markets—until after the fact. Owing to greater access to inside information, however, manager's forecasts usually are better than the markets' on average. Thus, financial managers should try to minimize the cost of financing from their point of view. But the correct financing choice requires a reliable view of the financial, and in particular, the stock market's opinion about the company's prospects.

Fortunately, the stock market itself can be used as a barometer of investor opinion about the company's image. The market value of a company contains an implicit assessment of corporate prospects on the part of all traders in the firm's shares. Management can attempt a fundamental appraisal of whether the company is worth its stock price. The difference between the managerial and market values provides an estimate of the expectations gap.

A related assessment is implicit in the proportion of the firm's value which the market associates with future growth. Breaking the total value of the corporation into two parts and then comparing the future growth value to the current earnings value permits an estimate of where the market sees the company in its life cycle (See Chapter 6.)

In general, when an expectations gap opens up, what can the financial manager do about it?

Alter Corporate Strategy and Expectations

The financial market's perception of the company's life cycle position and its value provides a provocative external reference point for the critical evaluation of the company's strategy. Before proceeding to explore the financial implications of a difference of opinion with the market, it behooves management to make sure that its own house is in order.

An expectations gap may reflect an error on the part of management rather than the market. Management's expectations may be unrealistic; the corporate strategy may be inconsistent with the environment. If so, management should change its thinking rather than try to influence the market. Corporations with poorly defined strategies like the conglomerate diversifiers of the 1970s, for example, ignored the financial market's opinion at their peril.

An audit of the company's strategic position can be carried out by examining the actual quality of growth in each of the firm's major subdivisions. Is each subdivision creating value in the sense that its strategy is supported by a long-run return on investment (including the synergistic and spin-off benefits of interaction with other parts of the firm both currently and in the future) which is greater than the shareholders' opportunity cost of the funds tied up in the division? While it is important not to underestimate the returns on current business activities, it is equally important not to write off an apparently low stock market price as meaningless, before ensuring that the existing strategy can withstand critical evaluation.

The U.S. international banking industry, for example, had mid-1983 price earnings ratios which were only half the market average, well below their traditional level. Investors were concerned about the security of developing country debt. On the basis of their public pronouncements, bankers believed the problem could be managed. However, the growing politicization of international debt rescheduling suggests that the market's estimate of bad-debt write-offs turned out in the end to be more correct than the bankers'. The financial expectations gap between the banking industry and the stock market was more symptomatic, therefore, of a fundamentally weak strategic position, rather than a case of poor financial marketing on the part of the banks, or a pricing error on the part of the market.

Focus the Company's Image
with Financial Marketing

Corporate image advertising, despite the difficulty of measuring whether it has any impact, accounts for well over $1 billion in annual U.S. media expenditures. One controversial attempt to test the statistical link between corporate advertising and stock prices did find a positive impact; about 4 percent of the fluctuation in stock prices could be attributed to corporate advertising expenditures.

New product announcements and labor productivity were found to be the most effective advertising themes in terms of stock price impact. By contrast, sales and earnings growth as themes had little impact. This is not surprising, because the financial markets are not easily fooled. A marketing campaign that does not focus on previously undisclosed and relevant information is unlikely to have much effect on the cost of financing. Analysts prefer straight shooters: "It serves analysts and investors over the long run for companies to be straightforward, to tell us they made a mistake and not to try to hype a stock unnecessarily," says Merrill Lynch's Vogel.

Even for straight shooters, however, altering the financial image of a company is not necessarily easy. Unilever, one of the 20 largest industrial companies in the world, began its U.S. investor relations effort in 1979 after the $485 million acquisition of National Starch and Chemical Corporation. Several years of presentations and visits to security analysts and their meetings made only a small impact on the company's U.S. shareholdings. What did make a difference, however, was a security analysts' meeting at Unilever House itself in London, which featured two days of conferences with top management and one day touring a nearby R&D facility. The analysts were most impressed by detailed information on Unilever's favorable market share relative to its competitors, information which was not readily available in the United States. "Right after the meeting, two analysts who already followed Unilever published reports . . . (and then) two highly respected household products specialists who hadn't written up the company before, came out with mildly enthusiastic reports recommending purchase." This had a snowball effect and by the end of the year, U.S. investors held 16 percent of the stock, compared with 6 percent twelve months earlier, while the price increased ten points.

The possible benefits of disclosing more information than required by legal and accounting practice depend in the short run on the size of the expectations gap and the estimate of external funding needs. When both the gap and the funds needed are large, then so are the informational cost benefits associated with disclosure. The cost of additional disclosure, on the other hand, varies with the structure of the industry, tending to be greater in competitive than in monopolistic environments.

In the case of IBM's personal computer, the competitive costs of disclosing the approach to the new product line were very high. Moreover, the financial benefits were small, because the company did not require new external financing and any short-term increase in the stock price had to be weighed against the competitive costs of disclosure. Management, thererfore, chose to ignore the financial market's opinion of the company at that time and allow subsequent events to speak for themselves.

The economics of financial marketing are likely to be especially favorable when firms engage in fundamental repositioning. The creation of strategic focus by divestiture, for example, may create substantial confusion in the minds of analysts. Under these circumstances, explanation of the detailed strategy can help to correct a distorted image. This is also true for other repositioning strategies involving the expansion into new markets, say, or the shift from older capital-intensive to newer high-technology industries.

To communicate the (new) strategy, the information content of the marketing campaign needs to be orchestrated across all the available channels of communication: annual report, financial press releases, presentations at security analysts' meetings, as well as corporate image advertising. When the objective is to provide input into the market's determination of the company's stock price, the campaign should highlight the business and financial attributes which affect stock price: how the strategy is reflected in the level and risk of the cash flow, its anticipated growth rate, and the amount of investment required to sustain that growth rate.

An example of what a well-conceived financial marketing effort can achieve is provided by the experience of Philips. At the beginning of 1983, only 3 percent (five million shares) of the European side of the company was held by American investors at a share price of $7. After a United States tour involving 21 presentations in New York, Boston, and Chicago, providing information of which, the company believes, U.S. analysts and investors were unaware, the share price climbed to $20 in June 1983 and the number of shares held by Americans to 25 percent (47 million) by November 1983. The role played by other factors in the share price rise is, of course, difficult to separate out, but the financial marketing campaign did broaden the U.S. investor base, thereby allowing Philips to benefit from the bullish U.S. perception of high-technology companies.

Exploit the Expectations Gap

In pursuing the minimum cost of financing, management should select those financial clienteles from whom it believes the company can get the best value for the future stream of cash flows. Thus, the choice between debt and equity should reflect management's perspective on the relative valuation of the firm's financing instruments. When management is more optimistic than the market about the equity value of the company's future growth, it can shift the capital structure toward more debt, provided the company is not far from its target capital structure. During the late 1970s, when IBM's nominal market value after substantial earnings and asset growth was less than it had been a decade earlier, the company issued debt and repurchased stock. IBM's management gave as a reason its belief that the company's stock was undervalued. Although at the time the market was unimpressed, subsequent events have proven management correct.

Conversely, when management is more pessimistic than the market and believes the company's equity is overvalued, it can shift the capital structure in the other direction toward more equity. Levitz Furniture effectively followed this approach when its stock was selling at a market-to-book ratio of more than 10 during the early 1970s. The real growth required to justify the market's valuation of the company was simply not available, given the size of the furniture market at that time. The chairman of the company, not surprisingly, declared his preference for continued equity financing.

There is a caveat, however. For firms with a distorted financial image, the benefits of reducing the financial expectations gap must be weighed against possible negative effects on other factors influencing capital structure. Exploiting the expectations gap by means of debt financing may strain the company's debt capacity and reduce its financial flexibility. Conversely, retained earnings and equity financing may result in the forfeiture of tax advantages associated with corporate debt.

By the same token, however, the notion of a target capital structure must be treated with caution. Only the most visible, highly researched companies, with a stable image, can afford to ignore the information costs of financing. For other companies, the minimum-cost capital structure will vary with shifts in the expectations gap, as the company's financial image changes over the corporate life cycle.

Arbitrage Expectations Across Markets

More and more frequently the expectations gap between management and financiers is not uniform across markets. A company like Novo may be in the spotlight in one market, but in the shadows in another. Numerous European companies have been implementing this principle by capitalizing on the periodically more bullish sentiment in the U.S. equity market. Three examples have been mentioned: Unilever, Philips, and Novo Industrii. These illustrate the opportunities for reducing financing costs that come with multiple stock exchange listings.

The difference in attention and expectations between markets provides an ideal setting for the use of a swap. Swaps provide a way of exploiting differences in perceptions across markets. More specifically, swaps arbitrage different levels of risk and visibility between the short-term credit and long-term capital markets, or between different currency markets. The phenomenal increase in swap activity demonstrates that many if not most financial managers are aware of the opportunities. However, swaps are of no use to firms in the shadows of all markets. To employ a swap, a company must be in the spotlight in at least one market. Otherwise it has nothing to offer the other party. Moreover, swaps are restricted to instruments with predetermined cash flows. They cannot be used for equity, since shareholders are unlikely to agree without a vote to an exchange of ownership.

INTERNATIONAL FINANCING PATTERNS

In concluding, it is worth asking whether the shadow cost of financing is consistent, not only with anecdotal evidence, but also with statistically observed financing patterns. Numerous studies have been made of the determinants of corporate debt ratios, for example. Although there is disagreement about the importance of variables like company size, growth, profitability, risk, and industry in explaining debt ratios, virtually all observers agree on the importance of the country factor. But no satisfactory explanation has yet been given for why the national location of a company should affect its debt-to-equity ratio.

The shadow cost of financing provides a possible explanation. Countries with weak or nonexistent disclosure requirements and with a tradition of corporate secrecy can be associated with a larger neglected firm effect and, hence, a greater scarce information premium. As a result, public financing is less frequent. The main forms of financing are retained earnings and bank debt. To reduce the scarce information premium, the company's relationship with its key bankers has to be much closer. Over time, therefore, bank financing plays a more important role than in more informationally open environments. The amount of bank financing needed varies with the growth rate and the retained earnings available. But in the long run, whenever external financing is needed, the lowest information cost alternative is bank debt. If it is assumed that growth and retained earnings differences average out in the long run, it follows that average debt ratios should decrease with the degree of informational openness in the country's financial markets.

The available data is loosely consistent with this hypothesis. Although national preferences for secrecy are difficult to measure, the largest countries can be ranked on the basis of common perceptions of their financial openness. Disclosure requirements, financial accounting and reporting standards, the strength of the financial media, all have given the U.S. markets the image of being the most informationally open. The U.K. market is generally regarded as somewhat less open. By contrast, the German market, with far less stringent disclosure and reporting standards, reflects a much greater penchant for secrecy. Although the Japanese market appears to be more open than the German market based on the scope of the available financial statistics, the Japanese have the strongest preference for personal contact and long-term relationships in their financial dealings. Thus, bank financing in Japan often takes on some of the characteristics of equity, especially with respect to the long-term risk assumed by the banks.

Taken together, this suggests that the scarce information premium and thus the advantages of bank financing, increase as one moves from the United States to the United Kingdom, to Germany, and Japan. Available data indicates that average long-run debt ratios also increase in the same order: for example, the average debt ratios were estimated as follows in 1964/1965: United States, 38 percent; United Kingdom, 45 percent; West Germany, 50 percent; Japan, 72 percent; in 1979/1980: United States, 54 percent; United Kingdom, 55 percent; West Germany, 60 percent; Japan, 78 percent.

In contrast to the scarce information premium, there is no evidence of a systematic (consistently positive or negative) expectations gap between management and the capital markets, or between national capital markets. Since the sign of the expectations gap changes over time, it does not consistently favor either debt or equity. In the long run, therefore, the information cost of financing associated with expectation gaps should not affect average debt ratios.

But might not the patterns associated with the shadow cost of financing merely be manifestations of segmented capital markets? Will they not gradually disappear as the markets become more globally integrated? Greater capital market integration is likely to reduce the magnitudes of the expectation gaps across countries, but not periodic expectation gaps between management and the markets, which are likely to persist owing to the economics of information disclosure. More importantly, the economics of security research will ensure the continued existence of a neglected firm effect and a related scarce information premium. As a result, the financial managers of neglected firms, in particular, will only be able to minimize capital costs by managing the shadow cost of financing.

BIBLIOGRAPHY

To simplify the reading of the text, we have avoided the academic habit of footnoting each page. Instead, this bibliography lists the sources of the studies cited, as well as other articles that we have found useful. Measures of statistical significance were also excluded from the tables in the text. Readers interested in this information should refer to the corresponding articles below.

R. AGGARWAL, "International Differences in Capital Structure Norms," *Management International Review*, Vol. 21 (1981).

E. I. ALTMAN, "Financial Ratios, Discriminant Analysis and the Prediction of Corporate Bankruptcy," *Journal of Finance* (September 1968).

AVNER ARBEL, *How to Beat the Market with High Performance Generic Stocks*. New York: New American Library, 1986.

AVNER ARBEL and PAUL STREBEL, "The Neglected and Small Firm Effects," *The Financial Review* (November 1982).

AVNER ARBEL and PAUL STREBEL, "Pay Attention to Neglected Firms," *Journal of Portfolio Management* (Winter 1983).

AVNER ARBEL, STEVEN CARVELL, and PAUL STREBEL, "Giraffes, Institutions and Neglected Firms," *Financial Analysts Journal* (May/June 1983).

JOHN ARGENTI, *Corporate Collapse: The Causes and Symptoms*. London: McGraw Hill, 1976.

ROLF BANZ, "The Relationship Between Return and Market Value of Common Stocks," *Journal of Financial Economics*, Vol. 9 (1981).

CHRISTOPHER BARRY and STEPHEN BROWN, "Differential Information and the Small Firm Effect," *Journal of Financial Economics*, Vol. 13 (1984).

CHRISTOPHER BARRY and STEPHEN BROWN, "Limited Information as a Source of Risk," *Journal of Portfolio Management* (Winter 1986).

SANJOY BASU, "Investment Performance of Common Stocks in Relation to Their Price—Earnings Ratios: A Test of the Efficient Market Hypothesis," *The Journal of Finance* (June 1977).

W. SCOTT BAUMAN, "Investment Experience with Less Popular Common Stocks," *Financial Analysts Journal*, Vol. 20 (1964).

W. SCOTT BAUMAN, "The Less Popular Stocks versus The Most Popular Stocks," *Financial Analysts Journal*, Vol. 21 (1965).

V.S. BAWA, "Optimal Rules for Ordering Uncertain Prospects," *Journal of Financial Economics*, Vol. 2 (1957).

PAMELA BAYLESS, "The Art of the Product Launch," *Institutional Investor* (June 1984).

WILLIAM BEAVER, "Fundamental Ratios as Predictors of Failure," Empirical Research in Accounting: Selected Studies, *Supplement to Journal of Accounting Research* (1966).

PHILIP BROWN, DONALD KEIM, ALLAN KLEINDON, and TERRY MARSH, "Stock Return Seasonalities and the Tax Loss Selling Hypothesis: Analysis of the Arguments and Australian Evidence," *Journal of Financial Economics*, Vol. 12 (1983).

ARTHUR BURNS and WESLEY MITCHELL, *Measuring Business Cycles*. New York: National Bureau of Economic Research, 1946.

STEVEN CARVELL, "The Impact of Analyst Neglect on Stock Market Performance," Ph.D. dissertation, State University of New York at Binghamton, 1984.

STEVEN CARVELL and PAUL STREBEL, "A New Beta Incorporating Analysts Forecasts," *Journal of Portfolio Management* (Fall 1984).

STEVEN CARVELL and PAUL GRIER, "The Small Firm Effect, Systematic vs. Total Risk and Implications of Diversifiable Risk for Small Firm Portfolios," working paper, 1985.

STEVEN CARVELL, ROBERT PARI, and TIMOTHY SULLIVAN, "The Determinants of Price Earnings Ratios," Working Paper, Bentley College, Massachusetts, 1986.

STEVEN CARVELL and PAUL STREBEL, "Is there a Neglected Firm Effect?" *Journal of Business Finance and Accounting* (1987). Forthcoming.

JAMES B. CLOONAN, "A Matter of Opinion," *AAII Journal* (January 1985).

KALMAN COHEN, GABRIEL HAWANINI, et al., "Friction in the Trading Process and the Estimation of Systematic Risk," *Journal of Financial Economics*, Vol. 12 (1983).

L. M. COLLINS and WILLIAM SEKELY, "The Relationship of Headquarter Country and Industry Classification to Financial Structure," *Financial Management* (Autumn 1983).

KARE DALLUM and ARTHUR STONEHILL, *Internationalizing the Cost of Capital*. New York: John Wiley and Sons, 1982.

ASWATH DAMODARAN, "Economic Events, Information Structure, and the Return Generating Process," *Journal of Financial and Quantitative Analysis* (December 1985).

ELROY DIMSON, "Risk Measurement when Shares Are Subject to Infrequent Trading," *Journal of Financial Economics*, Vol. 7 (1979).

BARBARA DONNELLY, "The Perils of Multimarket Offerings," *Institutional Investor* (October 1984).

DAVID DREMAN, *Contrarian Investment Strategy: The Psychology of Stock Market Success*. New York: Random House, 1979.

DREXEL, BURNHAM, LAMBERT, INC., *Research Concentration in the Standard and Poors 500*, New York (1977).

ROBERT EDMINSTER and CHRISTOPHER JAMES, "Is Illiquidity a Bar to Buying Small Cap Stocks?" *Journal of Portfolio Management* (Summer 1983).

EDWIN ELTON, MARTIN GRUBER, and MANFRED PADBERG, "Optimal Portfolios From Simple Ranking Devices," *Journal of Portfolio Management* (Spring 1978).

EDWIN ELTON, MARTIN GRUBER, and MUSTAFA GULTEKIN, "Expectations and Share Prices," *Management Science*, Vol. 27 (September 1981).

GEORGE FOSTER, *Financial Statement Analysis*. Englewood Cliffs, N.J.: Prentice-Hall, Inc., 1978, Chapter 14.

JACK FRANCIS, *Investments: Analysis and Management*. New York: McGraw Hill, 1976.

WILLIAM FRUHAN, *Financial Strategy: Studies in the Creation, Transfer, and Destruction of Shareholder Value*. Homewood, IL: Richard D. Irwin, Inc., 1979.

XAVIER GILBERT and PAUL STREBEL, "Developing Competitive Advantages," *Strategic Management Handbook*, Warren, Gorham and Lamont (1986).

XAVIER GILBERT and PAUL STREBEL, "Outpacing Strategies," *Journal of Business Strategy* (1987).

BENJAMIN GRAHAM, D. L. DODD, and S. COTTLE, *Security Analysis: Principles and Techniques*. New York: McGraw Hill, 1962.

WILLIAM HALL, "Survival Strategies in a Hostile Environment," *Harvard Business Review* (Sept/Oct 1980).

ROGER IBBOTSON and REX SINQUEFIELD, "Stocks, Bonds, Bills, and Inflation: The Past and Future," *The Financial Analysts, Research Federation*, Charlottesville, VA. 1982.

Institut pour l'Etude des Méthodes de Direction de l'Entreprise (IMEDE), Pakhoed Holding N.V. Case (B), 1976.

CATHRYN JAKOBSON, "Creating an Industry of One's Own," *Institutional Investor* (1983).

ROBERT JARROW, "Jump Risks and the Intertemporal Capital Asset Pricing Model" *Journal of Business*, Vol. 57 (July 1984).

DONALD KEIM, "Size Related Anomalies and Stock Return Seasonality: Further Empirical Evidence," *Journal of Financial Economics*, Vol. 12 (1983).

H. LATANÉ and C. P. JONES, "Standardized Unexpected Earnings—A Progress Retort," *Journal of Finance*, Vol. 32 (December 1977).

PAUL LAWRENCE and DAVIS DYER, "Towards a Theory of Organizational Adaptation and ReAdaptation," Appendix in *Renewing American Industry*. New York: Free Press, 1983.

HIAM LEVY, "Equilibrium in an Imperfect Market: A Constraint on the Number of Securities in the Portfolio," *American Economic Review* (September 1978).

BURTON MALKIEL, *A Random Walk Down Wall Street*. New York: W. W. Norton & Company, 1973.

BURTON MALKIEL and JOHN CRAGG, "Expectations and the Structure of Share Prices," *American Economic Review* (September 1970).

HARRY MARKOWITZ, *Portfolio Selection: Efficient Diversification of Investments*. New York: John Wiley, 1959.

MORTON MILLER and FRANCO MODIGLIANI, "Dividend Policy, Growth and the Valuation of Shares," *Journal of Finance* (October 1961).

S. FRANCIS NICHOLSON, "Price-Earnings Ratios," *Financial Analysts Journal* (July/August 1960).

S. Francis Nicholson, "Price-Earnings Ratios," *Financial Analysts Journal* (January/February 1968).

Jaye Niefeld, "Corporate Advertising," *Industrial Marketing* (July 1980).

Robert Pari and Son-Nan Chen, "Estimation Risk and Optimal Portfolios," *Journal of Portfolio Management* (Fall 1985).

Thomas Peters and Robert Waterman, *In Search of Excellence: Lessons from America's Best Run Companies.* New York: Harper and Row, 1982.

Thomas Piper and William Fruhan, "Is Your Stock Worth Its Price?" *Harvard Business Review* (May/June 1981).

Michael Porter, *Competitive Strategy: Techniques for Analyzing Industries and Competitors.* New York: Free Press, 1980.

Marc Reinganum, "Misspecification of Capital Asset Pricing: Empirical Anomalies Based on Earnings Yields and Market Values," *Journal of Financial Economics*, Vol. 9 (1981).

Richard Roll, "Vas ist das," *Journal of Portfolio Management* (Winter 1983).

Garth Saloner and Paul Strebel, "The Effect of Trading Volume on the Analysis of Risk and Return," Presented at Eighth Annual Meeting of the Eastern Finance Association, October 1978.

Myron Scholes and J. Williams, "Estimating Beta from Nonsynchronous Data," *Journal of Financial Economics*, Vol. 5 (1977).

Paul Schultz, "Transaction Costs and the Small Firm Effect," *Journal of Financial Economics* (June 1983).

G. William Shwert, "Size and Stock Returns and Other Empirical Regularities," *Journal of Financial Economics*, Vol. 12 (1983).

William Sharpe, "Capital Asset Prices: A Theory of Market Equilibrium under Conditions of Risk," *Journal of Finance*, Vol. 19 (1964).

William Sharpe, *Investments.* Englewood Cliffs, N.J.: Prentice-Hall, Inc., 1981, Chapter 14.

William Sharpe, *Asset Allocation Tools.* New York: Scientific Press, 1985.

Michael Spence, "Capital Structure and the Corporation's Product Market Environment," *Harvard Institute of Economic Research*, Discussion Paper 898, June 1983.

Hans Stoll and Robert Whaley, "Transaction Costs and the Small Firm Effect," *Journal of Financial Economics* (June 1983).

Paul Strebel, "Analysts' Forecasts in the Capital Asset Pricing Model," *Economics Letters*, Vol. 13 (1983).

PAUL STREBEL, "Using the Stock Market to Assess Strategic Position," *Journal of Business Strategy* (Winter 1983).

PAUL STREBEL, "The Stock Market and Competitive Analysis," *Strategic Management Journal*, Vol. 4 (1983).

PAUL STREBEL, "Managing the Information Cost of Financing," *Columbia Journal of World Business* (Summer 1986).

JAMES TOBIN, "Liquidity Preference as Behavior Towards Risk," *Review of Economic Studies*, Vol. 25 (1958).

NANCY WELLES, "How Unilever Got Noticed," *Institutional Investor* (June 1983).

VOLKERT WHITBECK and MANOWN KISOR, "A New Tool in Investment Decision Making," *Financial Analysts Journal* (May/June 1963).

KENNETH WILSON and ALICE McNEELY, A computer simulation of Steven Carvell and Paul Strebel's Neglected Stock Strategist, Banner Software, Inc., 1984.

INDEX

SUBJECT INDEX

Shadow portfolio. *See* Portfolio, shadow
Shadows, information. *See* Neglect
Shareholders, number of:
  neglect and, 71–73
  popularity flow and, 154–55
Size, company:
  analysts and, 31, 38–39
  beta and, 55, 90
  impact of, 15, 25–28
  individual investors and, 15
  institutional investors and, 15, 34–35,
    38, 39
  January phenomenon and, 28–29
  jump risk and, 57–58
  listing period and, 36–38
  neglect and, 15, 25–28, 31, 34–35, 38–
    39, 40, 42, 172
  P/E ratio and, 25–28, 38
  performance and, 25–28, 39, 40, 42–44
  risk and, 25–26, 34–35, 57–58, 189,
    191
Spotlight, companies in the, 15–16
  risk and, 48–49
Standard deviation, 48
Standardized unexpected earnings
    (SUEs), 152–53
Statistical analysis:
  earnings estimates, 141–44
  fundamental analysis linked to, 146–47
  price-earnings multiplier model, 134–
    35, 137–39, 141
  utility of, 133–34
Stock splits, 153
Systematic risk:
  apparent discounts and, 59–60
  bankruptcy risk and, 99, 101
  beta coefficient and, 89–90
  definition of, 49
  environmental instability and, 87–89
  impact of jump risk on, 58
  measuring, 89–91
  new beat and, 91–92, 94
  of portfolio, 188–89
  shadow, 59, 87, 91–92, 94
  thin trading and, 73

Tax-loss selling, January phenomenon
    and, 28–29, 44
Technical analysis:
  popularity flow and, 159, 161–65
  role of, 62, 63
Thin (infrequent) trading, 73–75, 156–57
  beta and, 54, 55
  neglect and, 172
  systematic risk and, 73
13F reports, 78, 79
Trading:
  insider, 151, 153
  institutional, 73–74

large block, 73–74, 151
neglect and, 73–75
number of shareholders, 71–73
relative volume of, 73–75, 155–56, 158
thin, 54, 55, 73–75, 156–57, 172
Trend lines, earnings estimates and, 141–
    44

Uninteresting companies, 16

Valuation model:
  cash flow and, 112
  liquidation approach, 111–12
  ongoing-entity approach, 112
Variability, performance, 48–49
Volatility, performance, 48
Volume, relative trading, 73–75, 155–56,
    158

Yield, earnings, 25–26

Z-score model, 96–97

NAME INDEX

Brown, Philip, 28, 51–52
Brown, Stephen, 36–38
Brush-Wellman, 81
Burnham Service Corp., 80–81
Burroughs, 120, 125, 126, 127, 128–29

Carnation, 204
Carvell, Steven, 33–36, 38–39, 40, 42, 138–39, 147
Champion Sparkplug, 189
Chen, Son-Nan, 189, 191
Chicago-Milwaukee (C-M), 163–64
Chrysler Corporation, 23, 153, 177, 189
Commodore International, 98–99, 101–7, 120, 127, 129–30, 147, 194–96
Compustat, 80
  COMPUSTAT II, 80
Contrarian Investment Strategy, 23
Control Data, 120, 125, 126, 127, 128–29
Cragg, John, 135, 137
Cray Research, 18

Damodaran, Aswath, 47
Data General, 120, 125, 126, 127, 129, 143
Davis, Donald, 206
Deluxe Check Printers, 18
Digital Equipment Corporation (DEC), 18–19, 120, 123, 125, 126, 127, 129, 189
Disclosure, 79
  Disclosure II, 79
Disney, Walt, 18–19
Do-It-Yourself Research Institute, 206
Dow Jones Industrial Average (DJIA), 28
Dow Jones News/Retrieval service, 75, 83, 157
Dreman, David, 23
Drexel Burnham Lambert, 17, 83
Dun and Bradstreet, 96
Dyer, Davis, 102

Elton, Edwin, 66, 188–89
Equitable Investment Management, 12

Federal Communications Commission (FCC), 205
Federal Express, 18, 189
Forbes, 23
Francis, Jack, 133

Garcia, Beatrice, 18
General Cinema, 18
General Motors (GM), 56
Getty Oil, 189

Glantz, Ronald, 56
Gruber, Martin, 66, 188–89
Gultekin, Mustafa, 66

Halliburton, 18
Hasbro-Bradley (H-B), 159, 161–62
Hewlett-Packard, 18

Iacocca, Lee, 153
Ibbotson, Roger, 57
IBM (International Business Machines Corporation), 54, 72, 74–75, 78, 90, 118, 120, 121, 122–23, 125, 126–27, 128, 129, 143, 209–10, 211
I/B/O/L, 157
ICARUS Service, The, 82–83, 157
ICH Corp., 161–62, 163
Institutional Brokers Estimate System (I/B/E/S), 38, 82, 83, 120, 138, 153, 194
  I/B/O/L, 157
  "Monthly Comments," 139
  Monthly Summary Data Service, 144–46
Institutional Investor, the, 16
Internal Revenue Service (IRS), 71
International Royalty of Oil, 72, 78

Johnson & Johnson, 18
Jones, C. P., 152

Keim, Donald, 28
Kisor, Manown, 134–35, 137
Kleindon, Allan, 28
K-Mart, 18
Kurtz, Donald B., 12–13

Land of Lincoln Savings and Loan, 78–79
Land Resources, 78–79
Latane, H., 152
Lawrence, Paul, 102
Levin, Doron P., 56
Levitz Furniture, 211
Limited Stores, 18
Lintner, 114
Lockheed, 23
London Stock Exchange, 80
Lynch, Jones, and Ryan, Inc., 38

McDonald's, 18–19
Malkiel, Burton, 135, 137
Markowitz, Harry, 192